Social Science Frontiers

Occasional Publications Reviewing New Fields
for Social Science Development

The Corporate Social Audit

by Raymond A. Bauer
and
Dan H. Fenn, Jr.

Russell Sage Foundation
1972

Russell Sage Foundation
230 Park Avenue
New York, N.Y. 10017

Foreword

That business has a responsibility to society beyond the making of profits is now a commonplace, though still far from a universally accepted idea. Nonetheless in a climate of social responsiveness, as evidenced strongly in the late 1960's and projected to continue for some decades ahead,[1] it is important to note that the issue of corporate social responsibility has *not* generally polarized around profits on the one hand and social responsibility on the other,[2] which in itself may be an indicator of the changing business climate.

Actually the very *concept* of socially responsible business has existed at least since the era of the ancient Greeks who found offensive the notion that wealth was to be used as its owner pleased without regard for "the interests of humanity and of social consequences."[3] Medieval merchants found their business ethics couched in the language of the church: The justification for trade lay in the merchant's intentions; if his prime objective was profit, then he

[1] T. Gordon, et al., *A Forecast of Interaction between Business and Society in the Next Five Years,* Institute for the Future, R-21, April, 1971.
[2] Milton Friedman, *Capitalism and Freedom* (University of Chicago Press, 1962), notwithstanding.
[3] Karen Arenson, "Background Research on the Notion of Social Responsibility in Business" (Russell Sage Foundation, unpublished manuscript, 1971).

was sinfully engaged; his proper duty was to earn enough to live and to help the good of his neighbor. Money was only a means to an end and commerce was to be carried on honestly and well. With mercantilism and then industrialization, the social responsiveness of business changed as the nature and demands of society changed. Today three approaches to business's relationship to society are clearly identifiable.[4]

The first is that of "traditional" business and stems from the early industrial era: Business operates in a competitive market and functions to make profit, hence the businessman is required only to deal fairly and honestly with his clients. The question of how one makes a profit or for what purpose is not particularly germane to the businessman *qua* businessman. Those who are committed to this attitude and who do make contributions to the general welfare do so primarily by serving in community or charitable organizations.

The second view has been gaining ground since the turn of the century. This approach holds that business has a responsibility to society with respect to its employees and products, and a responsibility to mirror the ideals and values of the society within its own microcosm. Businessmen then act affirmatively to promote safety, honesty and efficiency; to contain and eliminate where possible those disruptions to the environment caused by their products or processes; and to create within their own institutions the conditions of nondiscrimination demanded by society.

The third viewpoint is an activist one. Currently it is held more by critics of business than by businessmen. It is a primary obligation of business to use its power to promote social ends perceived as moral—for example by refusing to sell to government unless the government withdraws from Vietnam or refusing to deal with other corporations whose services may further the prosecution of the war. (Other examples are South Africa or Angola.)

Those holding the traditional view rely on "market mechanisms" or government programs to resolve social issues. Direct action is often considered to be inappropriate—a diversion of management skills or a violation of responsibility to the owners. Those taking the second view find it desirable to address social problems aggressively within the scope of "normal business activities" (manufacturers exercising control of their pollution, minority recruitment

[4] See Gordon, *op. cit.;* John G. Simon, Charles W. Powers, and Jon P. Gunnemann, *The Ethical Investor: Universities and Corporate Responsibility* (New Haven: Yale University Press, 1972).

and training programs; financial institutions providing loans for pollution control, for the development of black businesses). The activist view seeks the use of corporate influence and action in social areas not usually associated with normal business functioning. (The latter is usually expressed via outside pressure tactics, such as the calling for a boycott of Gulf Oil by the United Church of Christ.) Within business, we find a telephone company sponsoring clinics on drug abuse, or a University voting its shares of stock on a political resolution unrelated to the conduct of a company's business.

Accumulated evidence suggests that in the past few years, corporate management and institutional investors, particularly, have become increasingly sensitive to demands for "social responsibility." What these social responsibilities consist of is yet to be definitively stated, but much has been said and much has been done. For example:

> From the Bank of America has come the recognition that business must "adjust to the realities of a new social and economic environment"; that a bank has a special obligation to be a catalyst to change; that the company has a "role to play in the process of solving contemporary ills"; and that "we expect to include such factors in our assessment of the potential performance of other companies, and we expect to be judged on the basis of such factors in the conduct of our own business." The Bank formed a committee on Social Performance Priorities which designated four areas for "accelerated" action: housing, minority rights, environment and social unrest.

> Ralph Nader's Project on Corporate Responsibility (Project GM); Alice Tepper's Council on Economic Priorities; Harvard's Committee on University Relations with Corporate Enterprise ("to recommend ways they can work together for constructive social purpose"); the Committee on Economic Development policy statement; mutual funds efforts to develop a "Code of Responsibility for Investment Companies"; the Dreyfus Fund Survey of its stockholders; and the initiation of the Third Century Fund.

A major question remains: How does one measure a corporation's social performance?

Much has been said about the general subject but little has been contributed to answering this fundamental question. Thus, in

November 1971, Russell Sage Foundation sponsored a development effort aimed at examining the "'state-of-the-art" and at suggesting a program of research that would advance that state.

Raymond Bauer and Dan Fenn have provided us with a first product—a state-of-the-art conception and description, and recommendations for future development. They are to be commended for their astute considerations and their clear thinking in the murky pond of corporate social audits. Their effort has provided the social science community with a point of departure for future research in the area.

Eleanor Bernert Sheldon

Contents

Introduction

This paper deals with what may be an emerging new social institution, the formal "corporate social audit." The concept, which has a thin history, indeed, began to appear in the past decade or so, though, of course, society has been making generalized judgments of business for centuries. But the past year has seen a literal explosion of interest on many fronts, some quite unexpected, all in the context of the new attention being paid to the "social responsibility of business." In its full vision, the corporate social audit should permit firms to report their performance on issues of current social concern with the same regularity that they report financial performance. But, as we shall see, there are many partial visions being explored today.

We mentioned that the modest flurry of interest of the last ten years is now beginning to look like a storm. From early in the autumn of 1971 when we started on this paper to mid-winter the change has been startling. Hardly a day goes by that we do not find new evidence of interest in the idea, or hear of a company that is either toying with or embarking on some project they call a "social audit," or a major investor expressing the hope that here may lie the answer to his worries over a "social portfolio," or a public interest group performing an "audit." All this talk and activity goes

1

beyond the kind of criticism of business that is characteristic of groups like Ralph Nader and his associates or Campaign G.M. The goal of the social audit movement is the mounting of a comprehensive and objective evaluation of the social performance of firms on a continuing basis.

We have no doubt about the viability of the more general issue of social responsibility. But no one, at this stage, can forecast with any confidence the future shape of this concept of a social audit. We do believe, though, that the society cannot long have one without the other, that our apparent dedication, or rededication, to a new definition of corporate responsibility demands and depends on some kind of "audit." Thus we regard the broad concept as a potentiality worth looking at and thinking about. Consequently we have set ourselves the task of learning from the meager and somewhat covert history of social auditing and by speculation and reasoning to sketch out some of the many guises it has assumed—for the term has been stretched to circus tent proportions—as well as the shapes it might assume and the uses to which it might be put. In addition we have explained the problems that may be associated with the various forms and uses.

Our ultimate objective is to outline a program of research and development which might be undertaken if the potential of the concept is to be developed. On the way to this goal, we will have a number of things to say that should be of guidance to the practitioner who is brave enough to try his hand at this new art form. In particular we investigate many of the methodological problems involved in converting what is now an abstract concept into operational procedures.

Corporate Responsibility in the 70's: Toward Definition and Measurement

Underlying much of the discussion of business responsibility today, be it cocktail party chatter or business conference speeches, is the chauvinistic assumption that concern with broad corporate social obligations is an American discovery dating from the late 1960's. Although there are clearly some important new aspects to the issue today which set it apart from earlier manifestations, this assumption is demonstrably inaccurate. Even a cursory reading of history shows that we are operating on a continuum which goes back at least as far as the ancient Greeks. Furthermore, a look at the concerns of businessmen and social philosophers of the past provides ample evidence that at least some of the thoughts being expressed today have very deep roots indeed.

For example, the captains of industry of Miletus and Priene were subject to intense criticism from the upper classes of their societies if they failed to practice a standard of morality in trade which went beyond common honesty, or if they failed to attend to the question of how they could use their wealth for the greater good. The Greeks were particularly offended by the suggestion that material gains from business were to be employed merely as the owner wished, without regard for the interests of the community

3

and without due consideration for the social consequences of the process by which the riches were acquired.

By medieval times, the church had been substituted for the general climate of operative opinion as the watchdog of the businessman. The emphasis was placed on the entrepeneur's motivations as the factor determining the appropriateness of his behavior —a point of view not much different from that taken by many of today's activists who seek to sharpen the business executive's sensitivities to their concerns. The church took on the responsibility for applying its standards of good and evil and the metes and bounds of acceptable commercial behavior. The line of demarcation was determined by a man's purpose in being in trade: if he was primarily concerned with making money for himself, he was sinfully occupied; if, on the other hand, he was fulfilling his own immediate needs and then occupying himself with his neighbor's welfare, he was conducting himself according to the teachings of the church. Money thus was only a means to an end. This principle, coupled with the requirement that commerce or trade be carried on honestly, was operatively and philosophically accepted.

In the seventeenth century, with the appearance of mercantilism, all this changed. Wealth was seen as a positive good in itself, and direct concern with the well-being of society, including one's work force, diminished. With the industrial revolution came the concept that competition should serve as the regulator and determinant of proper business conduct; if you survived and prospered you were, by definition, doing "the right thing," and "in the right way." The appeal of this view was and is compelling; it lives on today in the often expressed conviction that "the cash register is the final arbiter of our performance. If the customer does not like what we are doing, we find it out soon enough." "Safety doesn't sell" said the pre-Nader automobile manufacturer. "We give the public what it wants," says the broadcasting executive.

Thus an interest in the proper conduct of business and its relation to the society of which it is a part is hardly a new or a peculiarly American phenomenon. Nor is it true that business has until recently operated in a world apart from the rest of society; obviously it has always, in a rough sense, reflected the values of the community in which it was imbedded.

But it is true that the last twenty-five years in the United States have seen a particularly large outpouring of business pronouncements on the general topic. As a matter of fact, Professor Paul T. Heyne pointed out in 1968 "that businessmen have been among the

most strident proclaimers of the new social gospel, that they have
been major contributors to the literature and philosophy of social
responsibility, and that with near unanimity they have announced
their willingness to bear this burden" [Heyne, 1968]. So it did not all
start with Owen D. Young in the 1920's or Frank Abrams in the
1950's or Henry Ford II in the 1960's.

In postwar America, this discussion was carried on mostly by
businessmen and their academic kin. It was taking place against
a most comforting philosophic background: businessmen were
happily telling themselves and anyone else who would listen that
we in the United States had created a new kind of capitalism, a
human capitalism, which put the lie both to Lenin and to Jay
Gould. The Communists were wrong, we were told; the system they
were railing against in the developing nations of Asia and Africa
was, at worst, a mythical monster with Karl Marx as its Franken-
stein and, at best, a picture of a business system which was now
out of date. We had evolved, they said, a special sort of mixed
economic system—some called it a "people's capitalism"—that was
really fail-safe, and we had put a new breed of businessmen in
charge of it. The businessmen expressed pride in the fact that they
had turned their backs on the robber barons of the late nineteenth
century, and freely admitted that their forefathers had carried on
in an unconscionable way.

It should be pointed out, incidentally, that this was also a time
when the business community was extremely active in selling "free
enterprise." Many, if not most, of the country's largest business
corporations actively, almost frenetically, promoted a great campaign of inspirational speeches, car cards, outdoor posters, radio
"listener impressions," in-plant conferences, and institutional advertisements to the tune of more than $100 million anually.

But for many of the most thoughtful spokesmen, it was a new
kind of free enterprise. They were talking about building still loftier
mansions for American business and so were expressing great
interest in "corporate citizenship" and "business responsibility in
action" and "business statesmanship."

This preoccupation took many forms. One of the first was the
exploration of the relationship between business and religion.
Searching the pages of the *Harvard Business Review,* for example,
one finds the issues of the mid- and late fifties sprinkled with
a series of articles in this area. One of the most popular pieces the
Review ever ran was called "Skyhooks," by O. A. Ohman [1955],
then Assistant to the President, Standard Oil of Ohio. An interesting

and, in many ways, prophetic statement which sold nearly 200,000 reprints, "Skyhooks" chided the business community for its failure to give thought to the revision of its basic philosophy and purpose. Calling for a "spiritual rebirth in industrial leadership," Ohman went on to equate effective management with the practice of spiritual values. (Describing an ideal executive whom he knew, he said: "He feels that no one has a right to louse up a job—a point on which he feels the stockholders and the Lord are in complete agreement.") Thus were God and Caesar reunited on the pages of the *Harvard Business Review!*

Another focus was business and politics. Through the fifties there was a rush of interest, courses were set up on practical politics, there was a torrent of articles and speeches, corporate-supported and public affairs programs began to appear. It was during this period that the Effective Citizens' Organization (now called the Public Affairs Council), a kind of trade association for corporate public affairs executives, was established. The motivation for all this was, of course, mixed. But when Clarence Randall said "there can be no other objective for business in politics than to raise to the highest levels the processes of a liberal democracy," he found a ready audience among businessmen who were interested in their responsibilities outside the demands of the office [Fenn, 1959].

The most recent manifestations of "social responsibility" need no reviewing here. Suffice to say that Watts and Newark produced a new area for discussion and action. Rhetoric from businessmen and public officials alike called on corporate management to step in, where government had "failed," to solve the problems of Urban America once and for all. Ralph Nader, consumerism, ecology, minority problems, women's liberation, South Africa, misleading advertising, Campaign G.M., student and church activism all tumbled over one another seeking attention, to the point where the businessman of the seventies is caught up in a confusing turbulence of demands and charges and concerns, all marching under the umbrella of "social responsibility."

The fact that there has been continuing concern with and a multitude of expressions of the social responsibilities of business over the years should not however be permitted to obscure the fact that today we find ourselves in a situation markedly different from anything we have experienced in recent years. For, as many observers have pointed out, we are in the midst of a great shift of values in the United States, of which the campus revolts are merely the most obvious and flamboyant manifestations. A new willingness to speak up, a challenge to authority (not a rejection, but a demand for credentials other than titles and salaries), a demand for a better balance between man and nature, new awareness of human as opposed to material values, the insistence on a bigger and better piece of the decision-making action—these and other factors are being isolated, identified, and analyzed.

According to George Lodge these shifting priorities have eroded the assumption of business legitimacy, and public opinion polls readily demonstrate that he is right. Until 1969, business was generally supported as doing a good, well-balanced job in the public interest; in that year, the figures tilted against the corporations, and they have been going down ever since.

Why the appearance—or, more accurately, the popularity—of these attitudes and concerns? This is clearly not the place for that kind of analysis. Many reasons are being put forward: population growth; affluence; a sudden awareness of the finiteness of our resources despite our affluence[1]; the forcing on our consciousness of the problems of those left out of our system; the impact of instant experience and instant information through television; a realization, stimulated perhaps by Rachel Carson, of the fact of second- and third-order consequences; the enormous growth in education (60 million Americans are now engaged in full-time study); the transformation from a "privilege" to a "right" of such services as adequate medical care, advanced education, and economic security.

Along with the new values—as cause, or result, or both—have come new tools of social action. During more stable times, the wider community affecting business in two ways: through the market mechanism, and through the political mechanism. For the moment, a third effective method has been found and developed by some skillful charismatic leaders who are politically oriented but not primarily concerned with the passage of legislation. Their approach rests on a judicious combination of good timing, and on the use of publicity; it mixes legal suits, *ad hoc* investigations, dramatic charges, and demonstrations in appropriate proportions. Only in a time of public disaffection would this approach work: who listened to Stewart Udall and Congressmen Kenneth Roberts and John Kennedy in the early sixties when they were talking about

[1] This realization of the finiteness of our resources despite our unprecedented affluence was probably precipitated by the sudden demands posed by the Vietnam War just at the time when we had resolved to turn our resources to the solution of a wide variety of social problems.

clean rivers and auto safety and a consumers' bill of rights? But today, in a changed climate that has engulfed all of us, the new tools are operational.

This changed—or, better, rearranged—value structure and the emergence of new tools to enforce it are now having an impact on the American corporation in at least four specific ways: through the investment community, employee activity, student involvement, and customer concern. (We do not mean to neglect here the obvious fact that businessmen, like judges, Congressmen, housewives, and lawyers and all the rest of us are inevitably caught up in these changes.) Let us look briefly at each of these ways, because they are producing so much unrest and anxiety in modern board rooms.

Investment Community

More Money Managers Reconsider Their Role in Shareholder Voting; Some Institutions Now Buck Companies on Social Issues.
Wall Street Journal, April 21, 1971.
Investor Panel Favors Social-Minded Firm with Slower Growth.
Last week, Campaign G.M.'s Moore asked the 12 largest mutual
Wall Street Journal, May 14, 1971.
funds to develop standards for measuring corporate performance in the areas of pollution and discrimination. It also asked the Investment Company Institute, the funds' trade association, to formulate a "Code of Responsibility for Investment Companies."
Business Week, May 1, 1971.[2]
My position with one of the larger institutions has led me to consider the responsibilities of the institutional investor. Should he permit any short-run earnings reduction to improve the probable long-term economic gain of his institution and of society?
William C. Greenough, *The New York Times*, May 2, 1971.
We are starting to pay attention to ecology because we think that the young financial analyst who is calling on us has it in the back of his mind. It never may become explicit in his reports, but we suspect it is going to affect them one way or another.
Corporative executive, May 1971.

These samples from a few weeks in 1971 testify to the increased attention to the investors' responsibilities and role. One of the earliest manifestations of the "social portfolio" was among some of the more liberal church groups concerned about the Vietnam War and the problems of American cities, but it has now spread far beyond such organizations. Campaign G.M. probably did as much as any activity to bring the issue to a head; the recent creation of special investment funds to channel money to "socially responsible

[2] This produced a statement of principles later in 1971 entitled "Corporate Responsibility and Mutual Funds."

8

companies," the 1971 SEC ruling that requires reporting of actual or pending litigation, and the soul-searching in college treasurers' offices are continuing manifestations. There is no reason to believe that social considerations deeply or widely affect investment decisions by individuals or institutions yet, but they are clearly higher on the agenda than they were only a few years ago.

Employee Interest

Current research discloses that the restlessness on college campuses today finds its counterpart, albeit muted and more polite, in many corporate structures. Judson Gooding found a virtual blue-collar revolt on automobile assembly lines; a major insurance company was troubled by the questioning its employees were doing about the socially beneficial nature of much of its product; a utility was under great pressure from its workers who felt that it was not serving its customers adequately; company after company in the defense business has ben attacked by its own employees for participating in the Vietnam War; Polaroid faced a deeply angered minority over its involvement in South Africa. In addition to their concern with the quality of their own lives on the job, and their input into corporate decisions that affect them, many employees and managers are questioning the social usefulness of what they and their employers are doing in American companies today.

Student Activism

The fascination of businessmen with what has been going on in colleges during the past few years has been an often-noted but little-discussed phenomenon. Until 1971, unrest on the campuses would almost surely excite interest and speculation, along with anger, on the part of executives, and articles on what the corporation should do about it appeared in many publications.

Why was this so? Perhaps for several reasons: many of the young people involved in the upheavals were sons, daughters, or friends of business leaders; the whole scene was so shocking as to demand some explanation; there was a deep-seated ambivalence in much of the corporate reaction for many felt that "those kids really do have something"; and executives were wondering what, exactly, would happen when this generation appeared at the desks and production lines in their companies.

Even though we have now had two years of apparent calm (actually, reported incidents are about as high today as they were two years ago, but press coverage is sparse and the more prestigious and attention-getting universities are far quieter), groups of students in colleges and graduate schools are spending a considerable amount of time thinking about and discussing corporate social responsibility. Many of them are seeking—and getting—interviews with top executives to present their views and, hopefully (as they see it), persuade managers to rethink and refeel their basic attitudes and motivations.

Customer Interest

We are beginning to see evidence of customer interest in the social performance of companies. M.I.T. recently shifted paper suppliers on the basis of a pollution report; a West Coast study [Kassarjian, 1971] reported that the impact of Chevron's announcement of an anti-pollution additive was very great despite increased costs; and corporate advertising, which is to some degree a reflection of consumer attitudes, is stressing social concerns and activities.

But beyond specific examples, at least one marketing specialist is reviewing the implications for the entire premise on which modern American selling is based. In the words of Lawrence P. Feldman [1971],

"To date, societal satisfaction has had either a residual or a negligible influence on consumer purchasing behavior. However, there are currently numerous indications that societal considerations will assume great importance as consumers begin to understand the resource implications of product use."

Further:

"There are indications that a growing segment of young American people are rejecting the idea that material consumption is an indication of social worth. This is particularly true in regard to consumption that involves goods associated with some adverse environmental effects. If the trend continues, the ethic of conspicuous consumption that underlies much of contemporary middle-class consumption behavior will be regarded with the same distaste in the future as today's generation regards the lavish displays of wealth exhibited by the nouveau riche at the turn of the century."

It is important to observe that none of these channels of community pressure for more (or different) social responsibility has, by itself, demonstrated great power or widespread effectiveness as yet. But relying on that fact as evidence that the whole thrust is not "for real" is akin to the Chrysler Board member who said, just a

10

few months before the Auto Safety Bill passed and a few months after *Unsafe at Any Speed* was published, that the whole issue was trumped up because "no one raised it at our annual meeting last week." "Change in psychological motivations always precedes economic and social change; consequently organizations will evolve in a direct relationship to the prevailing values, motivations, and desired purposes," says John F. Mee [1971]. The change in psychological motivations is certainly present; the tools, new and old, for the expression of that change are present; and the businessman knows it.

So the major new element that has been built into the equation in the last few years is this: the preoccupation with social responsibility, which has been the plaything of the business community since World War II, has suddenly become a meaningful and important—and even angry—topic of conversation in the community at large. This means, in practical terms, that the business manager no longer has the sole right and prerogative to determine just what kind of corporate behavior is socially responsible, and how much of it he must undertake to be a business statesman. Those decisions are being lifted out of his hands, in whole or in part.

It is small wonder then that the subject, once a soul-satisfying one for businessmen, has become instead a carrier of great anxiety. Under such circumstances, the business executive is more to be pitied than censured. He never knows when or from what quarter the attack will come, he has few tools and little experience to determine the viability of this or that particular charge, and he has no way of defending himself because no one, least of all the onrushing legions, has even any really useful measurements of performance or definition of social responsibility to tell him what he ought to be doing. More accurately, there is a wide range of definitions, none of which is widely accepted and consequently reliable as a guide to the practicing executive. There is, in short, no audit for an annual report.

It has often been pointed out that this is not the first upheaval of this kind, nor the first time that the once-accepted or even applauded practices of the business community have been swamped by a tidal wave of changed mores and standards. A new method of identifying such times has been supplied by E. L. Bernays in a recent history of the public relations profession which, he says, was started when, toward the end of the nineteenth century, "the unionists, Populists, Christian socialists and muckrakers were joined by the middle classes" in attacking businessmen for their insensitive ways [1971]. By the same token, the next high-water mark for the P/R consultants came with Franklin Roosevelt in the 1930's.

But just because this is not the first such moment in our history does not mean that it is the same as the others and will end in the same combination of strengthened legislation and more sensitive business leadership. It is at least possible, as some observers have suggested, that we are, without fully realizing it, redefining the nature and role of the corporation. In the past we have simply imposed new restraints on business; now, it is possible that we are fundamentally reviewing the role of business in American society.

The American corporation has been primarily a profit-generating, economically oriented machine because that is what we wanted it to be. It has attracted its financial support, its managerial talent, its public approval in direct ratio to its success in achieving the ends that we have set for it. Thus our expectations and our ideology have made the corporation what it is—not some inherent, inevitable, independent decision of its own. It really is a matter of "thinking makes it so"; and, almost magically, we will change the nature of a corporation by thinking of it differently. If, for example, we really took James Roche seriously when he said "profits and social progress must go hand in hand," and treated and rewarded the corporation as if we took him seriously, we would immediately find ourselves with another multi-purpose organization on our hands. The performance measurement process would change, both for executives and companies; the product would be different, the management style, the systems of incentives, the type of talent recruited and skills needed would also be different. It is not within the scope of this paper or our competence to speculate meaningfully on just what such a corporation would look like. The point is that if we are either consciously or unconsciously changing the corporation by redefining it, we had better think through carefully the implications of what it is we are doing. If we are to take George Kozmetsky [1971] at his word when he says "private enterprise and creative capitalism in their evolutionary process demand that profits become constraints rather than, as in the past, the primary objective," then we had better study Robert Briscoe's report [1971] of the confusion that ensued when a group of socially concerned managers tried to run a successful cooperative supermarket. In addition, given our continuing balance of payments problems, one cannot help but wonder if we indeed have all the flexibility we think we do.

Nevertheless, current intensity of interest seems to be supported by long-term social and economic trends. We report this as a fact of life albeit we are fully aware that the prevailing diffuse notions of what business should be responsible for will ultimately receive and fully deserve tight critical review and evaluation.

Our posture toward the concept of corporate social audits, let us remind the reader at this point, like our view of the related issue of corporate social responsibility, is clinical and neutral. Both exist, and to attempt to understand them does not necessitate that one regard them as either good or bad.

There are many features of the present drive for corporate social responsibility that are unquestionably marks of great progress. No one can doubt that we should no longer ignore the effects of pollution, or that women and minorities be given equal employment opportunities, and the like. Nor, more basically, can one argue that the great institutions of our society should brush aside the demands that they become more responsive to the changing mores of that society. But, there are many questions that will have to be answered. What are the proper roles of government, business, public interest groups, and special interest groups in defining the social conduct of business and social priorities in general? To what extent should business be responsive to an escalating series of demands from groups which may or may not reflect broadly held societal demands? To what extent does business have the resources to meet such demands without prejudicing its primary purpose of producing and distributing goods and services? To what extent are businessmen and business institutions equipped to serve the purposes that are being urged on them? Running a business has been a complicated matter under the simplest of circumstances. Can a businessman direct his affairs in a coherent fashion if he is pursuing a multiplicity of goals without any clear and enduring priority between them?

We make no pretense of answering such questions. We merely record them to document our awareness of their existence.

Be that as it may, the need for some sort of criteria for the social responsibility of business, some kind of definition of just what the words mean, some tools for measuring performance against that definition, has now become a matter of real urgency, and that fact, in our view, accounts for the lively current interest in the idea.

The social activists need a generally accepted definition if they are to make their charges viable; if they are to "improve" corporate performance, they need something more than a vague and subjective notion of what is "good" and a loose method of accounting. (One could, of course, say that looseness fits the needs of the reformers perfectly because they can evoke response from corporate management to any charge so long as they tag it social responsibility.) If the corporate executives are to improve their performance in this field, they too need to know what the field is and where the yardline markers are drawn. Even if they simply want to protect themselves from the complaints of customers and activists, they need such a definition. If the institutional and individual investors are to separate the socially responsible from the irresponsible, if they are to bestow white hats and black hats, they need definition and measurement. If customers are to buy selectively from the good guys and bypass the bad guys; if graduating students are to respond to the job offers from the responsible and reject the irresponsible; if students are to select their business targets with maximum efficiency and level their rifles at real bull's-eyes; if employees are to express their concerns meaningfully, they need definitions and measurements.

As one reads and listens and ponders today, it is surprising that we have not moved farther and faster beyond the stage of mouthing the term corporate responsibility and assuming that it has common and hard meaning. It becomes far less surprising, however, when one reviews both the literature on what has come to be called the social audit, understood as the attempt to define social responsibility and looks, even quickly, at the operating experience with it. But such advances require definition and measurements. Just what are the components of corporate responsibility, and how do you measure a particular company's performance in those components? How, in short, do you make a social audit of a business?

It is precisely at this point that we reach the thicket.

The Social Audit Today

Current Literature

There is available, of course, a great deal of written material which includes general definitions of social responsibility. Eels and Walton [1961], for example, interpret the term as dealing with those problems which arise when the corporate entity "casts its shadow on the social scene," and with "the ethical principles that ought to govern relationships between the corporation and society." They believe it represents a concern with the impact of the company on the individual, and also the recognized need for reconciling big business, labor and government with the deeply rooted values of our culture and form of government. Cheit [1964] quotes a leading oil company executive who defines the term to mean that the manager must realize his decisions will have consequences outside the confines of the company, and must pledge himself to try to make those private decisions in such a way that their consequences will accord with generally accepted values. Since every formal organization is a social system, Barnard explains, "it should give expression or reflect mores, culture patterns, implicit world asumptions" [1953]. In short, the bulk of the commentary has not gone much beyond the concept that there is a need to strike a balance between the interests of the corporation and the publics, including the general public, which it serves and with which it is associated. The implied role of the social audit idea is to explain and define this balance in particular areas of corporate activity and to describe the ways in which it can be achieved.

Note should be taken here of the view that this definition should be made by the government, rather than by the activists, the students, the investors, or the corporation itself. If corporations ought to be doing things they are not doing now, or ought to be doing things differently, some observers say, it is up to the government to tell them so in legislation and regulation. There are at least two difficulties with this approach: (1) governments are reactive, not pro-active, and the corporations and other interested parties who inevitably would be participants in the fashioning of the governmental decisions need guidelines and measures; and (2) while this may be the tidiest answer, the times have overtaken it since, in fact, everybody both inside and outside the business community is now engaged willy-nilly in playing the definition game.

Despite the growing use of the term social audit, the literature on the subject is remarkably thin. To the press, this may look like a simple business. According to Thomas Oliphant, writing in the Boston *Globe* in late May 1971:

> Almost all of this data exists right now on some corporate executive's desk. What is lacking is the decision to put it all together and release it to the public in a manner modeled roughly after financial accounting standards to ensure a maximum of information and a bare minimum of public relations . . . it [the social audit] has progressed far beyond the status of a vague idea.

One searches in vain for evidence that this is, indeed, so.

The discussion on the general topic, whether officially labeled social audit or not, falls into four categories, two of which merit some discussion. One approach is simply to collect evidence that a company is dong "no social harm," or is not currently under indictment by a governmental body. Another is to rely on the subjective impressions of knowledgeable and concerned people who have collected some data and talked with many observers.

The third is to take selected specific areas of activity and review them in detail. Probably the outstanding example of this approach is the Council on Economic Priorities which has devised a methodology for assessing a corporation's performance in such areas as air and water pollution and reporting on it. But there are others. Eastman Kodak recently ran an advertisement stating that

Currently our accountants and technical people are collaborating on devising methods to charge against a manufacturing department its contribution to the total output of solid, liquid or gaseous waste that must be rendered inoffensive to the outside world. The department superintendent whose cost-cutting lags in this added dimension may be regarded as pathetically in the superintendent's lunch club as the one whose material or labor costs are running away from him.

The Conference Board has devised a method for evaluating corporate public affairs programs which rates them according to whether or not they include some five specific components. The Equal Employment Opportunity Commission, along with many other private and public agencies, has worked out ways of recording and reporting performance in minority hiring and promotion.

Still another example of this approach appears in one of the earliest discussions of the social audit, an article by Fred Blum in *Harvard Business Review* in 1958. Blum's social audit was, essentially, an attitude survey taken at all levels of a firm to measure progress in human relations. Both "organization" and "individuation" were tested. Employees were asked to rate their overall attitude toward the company, their assessment of the competence of top management, their satisfaction with their position in the company, the fairness of the earning distribution, the adequacy of information, and the effectiveness of the organization as a whole. Further, they were questioned on their level of satisfaction in working for the firm and, specifically, their feelings about personal relations, pay rates, the use of their talents, and the nature of their jobs. Similarly, one of us developed a method for determining what the Boston Community thought of the social programs Boston companies were carrying out in the area. The general public, minority and ethnic groups, and officials of organizations, as well as corporate executives were surveyed. The business executives badly misperceived public expectations and assessment of their corporate giving, incidentally.

The fourth approach that appears in current writing is the attempt to develop sophisticated quantitative measures of social responsibility. Three examples are particularly worth recording for our purposes. LaPorte's measures of the impact of alternative technologies, Sater's three-dimensional matrix, and Abt's ambitious and comprehensive scheme for translating social goods into dollar values.

Todd LaPorte, writing in the *Public Administration Review* [1971], suggests a systematic study of all relevant relations in an attempt to measure the impact of technology. He offers a scheme for weighing technological alternatives in different areas as functions of the probabilities of achieving valued conditions such as certain political, social, psychological, and economic effects. He would weight the desired emphasis for each of these criteria according to social norms or expected norms, plug them into his function and use them to compare alternative solutions or technologies for achieving different goals.

Clair W. Sater, account adviser with Fields, Grant & Co., investment advisers, was Chairman of the Corporate Rating Project of the student-based Committee for Corporate Responsibility. Sater proposes that some external agency audit businesses on an industry-by-industry basis to supply ratings of corporate responsibility to be used by investors.

Sater lists a considerable number of dimensions along which firms might be evaluated: consumerism, type of international business, environmental protection, opportunities for minority group members and women, military and defense activity, contributions, and executive participation in community affairs. He quickly acknowledges that the relevance of these dimensions will vary from industry to industry, and suggests that the selection of dimensions be made of the basis of knowledge of particular industries. As an example, he proposes that a bank might be rated on the location, appearance, and desirability of its buildings, and on its policy toward lending to polluting industries.

Sater sees the difficulty in deciding how to weight a company that does well on one dimension and poorly on another, and concludes that the job of weighting should be left to the user of the audit. He also sees that all parties might not agree on whether such an activity as supplying munitions is a good thing or a bad thing, and suggests that the auditor may make his own evaluation, but conduct his ratings consistently so that the user can exercise his own judgment.

As sources of data, Sater proposes a variety of printed sources: government reports, local pollution agency reports, consumer agency reports, published speeches of corporate executives, federal equal opportunity reports, annual reports, articles in the business press, and the like. He also advocates the design of a questionnaire to be used in a fashion that is not entirely clear. Finally he would interview corporate officers to plumb their general attitudes on issues of social responsibility.

All of these data would be summarized in a five-point rating for each area of concern in a "three-dimensional rating matrix for an industry" which would make a company-by-company comparison according to various norms: other companies in the industry, other similar firms in the same geographic location, local legal requirements, and "the potential for action in areas where facilities are located." Investors would then take this audit into account in making their investment decisions. Figure 1 illustrates Sater's matrix.

The Sater proposal, which raises as many questions as it answers, is especially weak on the operational side. It is not clear, for example, how he proposes to use his questionnaire to gather "facts that are not obtainable elsewhere." He does not explain how the written sources he suggests would give adequate company-by-company coverage on all issues (for example, consumerism). At a minimum, to do this on a widespread basis, as he proposes, would constitute a prodigious task. We shall find that the new "socially responsible" mutual funds are proceeding along lines not too unlike what he proposes but on a somewhat more modest line. Furthermore, he bypasses the whole problem of the usefulness of such data in comparative audits.

While Sater's proposed audit is for the guidance of investors, Dr. Clark Abt of Abt Associates, Inc. offers an audit to be used by corporate officers in their own decision making.[3] He says it will produce the following immediate benefits: earnings increase, budgeting efficiency, early warning of opportunity and risk, positive public and governmental relations, and marketing improvements. His list of long-range benefits is equally long, and includes such items as "a rational basis for integrating corporate with national (including host nation) policy for maximum benefit of both." He would construct "a balance sheet of company current and long-term social assets and liabilities, and a statement of the social gains and losses in the current year." ["An Annual Social Audit."] By determining the dollar values of programs and their results, he would make an assessment of the effect of everything

---

[3] An early version of Abt's proposal "An Annual Social Audit" is reproduced in the *Congressional Record,* January 20, 1970, E111, E112. A later version is Clark Abt [1972].

FIGURE 1

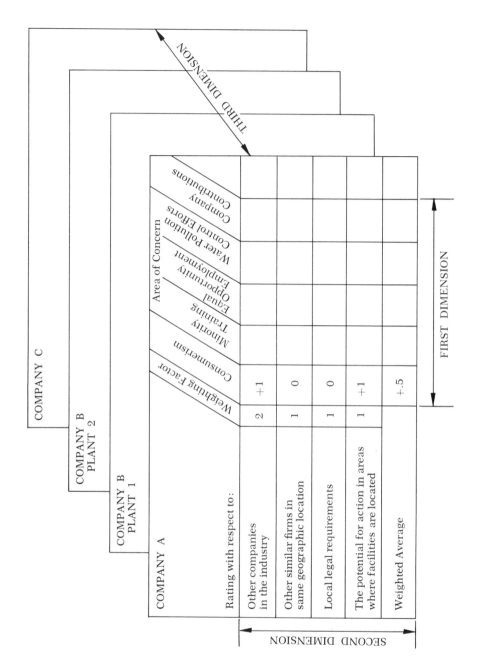

the company does or produces on the environment within which it operates. For example, he would establish what X company was costing the educational system of the community in which it was operating by calculating the investment the school system had made in each employee of the company and substracting the percentage of the corporate tax dollar which was going to support that school system.

From the description of Abt's proposal in the *Congressional Record* and *Innovation,* and from an undated manuscript, "How to Save Money by Doing Good," and "Social Audit" (a game for planning social investments), supplied us by Dr. Abt, we can piece together much of what he proposes. It is obviously a very ambitious plan for cost/benefit analysis of a company's actual and potential social programs. He would compute not only the out-of-pocket costs of social programs, but the opportunity costs of alternative programs foregone. He presumes that social programs are undertaken because they are in the long-run interest of the company, and by Abt's reasoning this contribution to the long-run interest can be translated in a dollar contribution to long-term profitability. This is what is promised in his documents.

Abt's documents are strong on the logic of his position, much of which is familiar welfare economics, but are less strong on making the contribution to long-term profitability—though they take steps in that direction. In one document ["Managing to Save Money While Doing Good"] he presents a plausible scheme for figuring the dollar value to society of a company's contribution to the Heart Fund. However, the merits of measuring health programs in dollar terms is a matter of hot debate in medical economics. Furthermore, if this goal is attained and one likes the results, the measure would be one of the contribution to the general welfare of the society. Presumably what benefits society will have some spillover benefits to the company that pays for those benefits. But, he does not show us how to convert such dollar benefits to the society into dollar contributions to the firm.

In another document ["Social Audit"], he goes a step further, and proposes that the benefits of a corporation's contribution to building a better community can be measured in terms of such things as reduced recruitment costs. In a small community where the totality of the factors contributing to its increased attractiveness could be identified, and the contribution of the company to that total isolated, this calculation is conceivable. For more complex communities, and/or other social programs, and/or benefits, it would be more difficult.

There is little doubt that systematic procedures, whether or not they be called social audits, could in all likelihood contribute to the efficiency of a company's social programs, and/or permit it to accomplish more with the same amount of money. As a matter of fact, Abt's audit of his own company did produce specific operational changes. Whether or not the contribution could be of the nature of magnitude of what Abt promises is another matter. We will discuss some the difficulties in a later section of this report.

In his article in *Innovation* Abt presents a scheme for a "Social Operations and Income Statement" (see Figure 2). Such a scheme would display a considerable amount of socially relevant information. It does not, insofar as we can see, yet relate to the profit benefits accruing to the company via its social activities. As we shall see in the next chapter, this scheme was the model on which Abt Associates built in conducting an audit of their own firm.

FIGURE 2.   SOCIAL OPERATIONS AND INCOME STATEMENT

Measure

(all costs in $1,000)

SOCIAL BENEFITS

Employees Compensation

Increases in per capita market value reflecting increases in productivity as shown by average salary increase	$
% of employees participating in increases reflecting scope of productivity increases	%
% increase in revenues per employee, reflecting per capita productivity increase	%

Fringe Benefits Affecting Quality of Life

Health

Health insurance coverage increases	actual & expected insurance payments
Life insurance coverage increases	actual & expected insurance payments
Employment & disability coverage increases	actual & expected insurance payments

Education

In-house courses: number, access	costs
Company-supported external program	costs
Number employees successfully completing courses by level & degrees	number

Recreation

Athletic program, company parties and outings	costs, in equipment space, man-hours

FIGURE 2.   SOCIAL OPERATIONS AND
INCOME STATEMENT (*continued*)

Measure

(*all costs in $1,000*)

Day care services	costs, in space, staff time, equipment, **R&D**
Food services	
Breakfast, coffee & snacks, at at-cost lunches	costs, & savings to staff of at-cost lunches & staff-time cost
Holidays and vacations	cost

QUALITY OF LIFE OTHER THAN FRINGES

Working conditions	
Work space/staff	ft²/staff, cost difference
Internal quality of work space	difference in taxes paid between our building & average in neighborhood & architects' costs
Air quality	cost of air-conditioning
Acoustic insulation & privacy	cost of added partitions, carpeting, curtains
Visual insulation & aesthetics	cost of trees, shrubs, grass, gardening
Parking at work	total daily parking cost, if paid by staff

CAREER ADVANCEMENT

Net promotions to positions of greater responsibility (e.g., promotions less demotions)	no., % of total, cost in salaries & fringes
Reputation net increase indicated by publications, and awards, public mention of staff at meetings, etc.	no., % increase, equivalent cost ($555/article)
Satisfaction indicated by *decrease* of voluntary terminations	no. reduced quits. $ value
Increased Employment	
Added number of jobs created	no. % increase in total payroll
Employment Security	
Reduced number & % of involuntary layoffs	no., %
Equality of Opportunity	
Minority Employment	
Minority employed (nonwhite & women)	no., % , $ salary & fringes
Ratio of minority total staff	% , % total salary
Minority Advancement	
Women given salary increases	no., % , total increased salary & fringes

FIGURE 2. SOCIAL OPERATIONS AND
INCOME STATEMENT (*continued*)

Measure

(*all costs in $1,000*)

Women promoted in management positions	"
Nonwhites given salary increases	"
Nonwhites promoted in management positions	"
Total minority given salary increases	"
Total minority promoted in management positions	"
Ratio of minority salary increases total salary increases	"
Ratio of minority promotions total promotions	"
Ratio of minority managers total managers	"

Environment

Environmental improvement (building, landscaping)	no., %, $
Reduced pollution	no., %, $

Public

Social impact of contracts	no., %, $
Contributions to knowledge	no., %, $
Public education	no., %, $
Awards	no., %, $
Unpaid services to public interest institutions	no., %, $

SOCIAL COSTS	Total Social Benefit

Employees

Staff-turnover	no., %, $ cost
Staff laid off	no., %, $ cost
Staff "free" time exploited	no., %, $ cost

Environment

Unfinished structure	no., %, $ to correct
Air pollution by power consumption	%, $ to correct
Recycle paper not used	no., %, $ cost
Driving to work causing air pollution	no., %, $ to correct
Water pollution	%, $ to correct

Public

Exploitation of local educational institutions	no., %, $ equivalent

NET SOCIAL INCOME (LOSS)	Total Social Cost

A final proposal is put forth by the Public Affairs Council [1971]. This proposal, in turn, is somewhat different than the others. The Council would also have the corporation carry out an audit with its own resources. It states the purpose of the audit in these terms:

The "INTERNAL CORPORATE SOCIAL AUDIT" is one device to which companies are turning to identify goals, to complement policy and to establish evaluative standards. The long-range goal of these companies is to institutionalize social concerns into the job of each corporate manager.[4]

The Council does not identify companies which are carrying out this practice.

The list of matters on which a company's social policies would be judged is long and detailed, and the criteria used for selecting these particular items and excluding others are unstated. Its scope can be garnered from the major topical headings: employment, supplier policies, advertising, contributions, voluntarism, government relations, trade association and other business-supported organizations. This list is marked by the amazing range of things for which the corporation would be held responsible. For example:

The company may need to allocate additional funds to the purchasing department to help develop minority suppliers. Technical assistance from the purchasing department is also needed to aid existing minority suppliers.

Advertising accounts are to be placed only in those firms with affirmative actions programs.

In line with corporate advertising objectives a minimum budget should be established for advertising in black and other minority group media.

Corporate function [sic] would be sponsored only at those private clubs which do not discriminate against any individual because of race, religion, or sex, etc.

Interestingly, the popular topic of pollution is not mentioned.

Thus the literature on corporate social audits is both sparse and diverse. If one takes the concept to mean what it seems to mean in the context of the present discussions—a systematic assessment of firms across a range of issues of social responsibility— then only the proposals of Sater and Abt would qualify. And even these two are diverse.

Perhaps the most important point in all this is that no unified

---

[4] This paper was circulated solely to stimulate discussion concerning methods of quantifying corporate social responsibility. It was not intended to be a model for a corporate social audit.

concept of what a corporate social audit is emerges from this literature, nor is there even any crude indication of common trends. And, as we turn to the next section, we shall find that firms which have been doing social audits have similarly diverse approaches.

Human Resource Accounting

The practice—or more accurately, the developing attempts at the practice—of social auditing has its forerunners in human resource accounting, developed at the University of Michigan by Professor Rensis Lickert and now operating under the direction of William C. Pyle, Director of the Human Resource Accounting Program[5] though the similarity is more ideological and methodological than it is substantive.

The core notion of human resource accounting is that human assets should receive the same treatment in accounting as do physical assets. One variant treats the hiring and training of personnel as investments rather than as expenses. The investments in turn should be amortized over their expected life, which may be assessed, either as the length of time that the employee will remain with the company, or the length of time that a skill will remain with the employee. This variant is employed by the R. G. Barry Corporation which has already used such data to report to its stockholders in a *pro forma* balance sheet which shows how the company's financial performance would look with and without an adjustment for an accounting of its human resources. The Texas Instruments Company uses another variant of human resource accounting, considering the *replacement* costs for groups of workers within different profit centers of the company.

There are extensions of human resource accounting which have already been tried in practice. One of them is to make social psychological measures of a work group and trace the predictive power of these measures over several years [Lickert & Pyle, 1971]. This approach treats employee morale and management practice as a corporate resource. Other more ambitious extensions are still in the programmatic stage. One approach would regard the firm's customers as a resource in which it has an investment, and periodically would audit the status of that resource: for example, the amount that has been invested in developing customer loyalty, and presumably the state of that loyalty.

[5] For a quick introduction of human resource accounting see Pyle [1970] and Lickert and Pyle [1971].

There is one point of apparent overlap between human resource accounting and corporate social auditing that highlights the comparison that might be made between the two. Both (as least in some versions of social auditing) would turn attention to the status of the employees, and might in fact ask many identical questions about their morale and management practices (see reference to Fred Blum, above). The *rationale* of human resource accounting is that this should be done because employee morale and management practices are an integral part of the future profit potential of the firm. The *rationale* of studying employee morale under the rubric of the corporate social audit is that in this day and age a company ought to provide a pleasant work environment and a creative work experience *even if* it does not contribute to, or despite its adverse effect on, profitability. (This is, indeed, one requirement for social responsibility which some activist groups and their adherents would establish.) It is true that there is a considerable amount of waffling around this latter rationale, with one uneasy person after another venturing the opinion that almost anything done to improve employee morale will contribute to the long (how long unspecified) range profitability of the firm. This, however, is undemonstrable.

If the intent of human resource accounting and of corporate social auditing is so clearly different in an area of common activity such as studying employee morale, why have we referred to the two movements as ideologically affiliated? Because even a superficial understanding of the people who developed the concept of human resource accounting makes it clear that many of their interests in the human side of things, and their concern that organizations serve people rather than *vice versa,* characterizes the present focus on social responsibility. While studies in the "human relations" tradition have demonstrated that the happiest employees are not always the most productive, one senses that the authors of such studies were most gratified when the two did coincide.

Aside from the ideological affinity of the two movements, human resource accounting has two direct implications for corporate social auditing. It represents an attempt to extend accounting methods beyond traditional financial accounting, and it has established some foothold in the accounting professions. It also shares with some aspects of corporate social accounting the use of social psychological measurement in an applied setting—though this practice extends beyond these two movements.

Some Current Efforts

Here we will review some of the concrete activities which are taking place in the name of social audits. Some of the components of these activities are, of course, familiar. Employee surveys have taken place for decades. Firms have been judged and have judged themselves on their hiring and advancement policies, on their pollution policies and practices, and so on. What interests us here, however, is a sample of instances which have come to our attention in which someone, either in a company or outside, is explicitly attempting the systematic assessment of firms or a firm on a range of social performance, and where it is presumed that this may be a recurring activity.

We should make clear that we are not including instances in which corporations have deliberately gone about setting general *policies* of social responsiveness. Rather we are looking at instances in which the *implementation* of present policies is being measured against some norm of performance, even if that norm be as subjective as the judgments and expectations of corporate personnel or of people being interviewed.

It is important to recognize that the amount of explicit activity along these lines is still small, and even that being undertaken is in its early stages. But the developing experience is producing both sufficient variety and sufficient regularity to be instructive. In the material that follows, we draw, first, on the work of four conventional business firms that are conducting audits.[6] Two of the firms are doing the audit with their own resources. One is working with a consulting firm, Arthur D. Little, Inc. and another is using an accountant as an outside consultant. In addition, Arthur D. Little is conducting an audit of itself, as is another consulting firm. Abt Associates.[7] Abt Associates has also carried out a partial audit for one unidentified client.

At this stage, the emphasis in these audits seems to be on internal use and decision making. The exception, Abt Associates, Inc., was designed for inclusion in their annual report. Nevertheless, one senses that most of these parties are entering into the enterprise with a high degree of tentativeness. They are feeling their ways

[6] For a preliminary report on one audit at ARA Services, see John J. Corson, "A Corporate Social Audit?," a discussion paper prepared for a Conference on The Corporation and the Quality of Life, organized by the Center for the Study of Democratic Institutions, September 1971.
[7] The Abt audit is completed and is reported in "1971 Abt Associates, Inc. Annual Report and Social Audit."

cautiously in every category from the methods to be used and the topics to be covered, to the use to which the information will be put.

Second, we have considered the experience of some other agencies that are beginning to audit firms. Two of them are new mutual funds created to offer investors a socially responsible portfolio, namely: The Dreyfus Third Century Fund and The Social Dimensions Fund. The first is already registered with the SEC; the second was not yet out of registration as of the end of 1971. (We have heard of more than a dozen similar efforts.) The other two are public interest organizations, The Council on Economic Priorities, and the Corporate Information Center of the National Council of Churches. (The former is in the process of branching out from the pollution focus mentioned above.)

Although we have interviewed one or more persons associated with each of these enterprises and have read a certain amount of public material we are handicapped in reporting on them by two circumstances: the unevenness of our knowledge across organizations, and the sensitivity of some of the organizations to information about their activities to this point. Accordingly, rather than aiming at systematic, comparative coverage, we will endeavor to put forth what we think we have learned. At points where it seems appropriate we will identify specific findings with specific organizations.

Self-Audits of Business Firms

We may first say that the idea of a social audit is not a burning issue for American business at large, but interest and curiosity about the idea are widespread. And, as we have indicated, the number of companies considering or engaging in some kind of effort which they call an audit is clearly on the upswing.

Nevertheless, as might be suspected, at this point the social audit is far from a standardized product. Its character is much a function of the industry, the particular circumstances of the firm in question, and the interests of top management. Even the two consulting firms, which have had between them one plus clients, have conducted the audits differently for the clients than they have for themselves.

These corporate self-audits can be compared on several dimensions: the dynamics behind them; their purpose; their scope; and their methodology. We shall now summarize what appears to be the current situation in these areas.

Popular belief to the contrary, firms undertaking a social audit

29

are not necessarily under fire. Rather, the determining factor seems to be the interest of a key person at the head of the organization who has a demonstrated history of social concern and innovativeness. (It is interesting to note that this is the major determinant in the role companies play in social activities generally.) This factor holds not only for the regular businesses but for the consulting firms as well. In two cases there was a partial or potential "threat" that affected the action, but that seems to have been a minor consideration.

The fact that this willingness to experiment with social audits is spearheaded by committed chief executives is important not only for our understanding of its origins but also for its subsequent progress. In not every instance are all of the members of the executive family equally enthusiastic. The process and outcome of the audit might take up their time and disturb regular operations; expose deep political and philosophical differences within the firm; usurp prerogatives (who has the right to see the personnel files?); create anxiety that new standards of evaluation are suddenly being applied; stimulate debate over tough issues like who should see the data; and reveal findings that may prove embarrassing if exposed to the public either deliberately or inadvertently. Further, in some decentralized companies it seems to smack of "headquarters" meddling and kibitzing. Thus in one company the work reached what was considered a sensitive stage just when the chief executive was about to go on leave of absence for a number of months. The officer in charge of the audit pushed it to the back burner, waiting until the the head man could give it his undivided attention, because one tentative attempt to audit one substantive area had ruffled the feathers of the heads of associated companies.

Though the origins of such projects may be with the chief executive, the motives vary. In some cases, it is simply a felt need for data. One might think that corporate officers would have a good idea of their areas of vulnerability. In fact, one of the purposes cited for undertaking these audits is precisely a feeling of anxiety at the lack of such knowledge. And some findings indicate this concern is warranted. One firm which never thought of itself as a "polluter" rather quickly realized that it was the source of a great deal of solid waste and a major dumper of detergents into our waters. Still another, also confident about its pollution record, discovered that the incineration it was doing was creating serious community concern. A third found that one of its operating divisions with a previously fine safety record had slipped virtually to the bottom of the group of several dozen companies with which it could meaningfully be compared.

(Incidentally, with regard to the internal conflicts caused by audits, one firm readily got safety records from one of its divisions which must regularly report such data to the Federal government. But, after several months, another of the divisions had not yet supplied the requested data.)

When one stops to think about it, this lack of information is not so surprising. There has been little reason or incentive for corporate officials to report such activities or even catalogue them, much less to pass information on their failures up the line. Since these activities have not been relevant data for evaluation and promotion, they have not shown up in the offices of top management except on a very hit-or-miss basis.

A popular cynical view of self-auditing is that the results will be used for public relations. It seems to us a better guess that in the near future the findings will be rather closely held until management has digested their implications and/or had the opportunity, if they so choose, to correct their areas of vulnerability. This is not to say that concern over vulnerability is the main motivator for audits. Generally the purpose is stated more positively as one of assessing the costs and benefits of social programs, employee status, relations to customers and the wider community, and of making trade-offs among social programs and between social programs and regular business. However, the potential embarrassment of adverse findings coupled with uncertainties as to just what internal decisions will be made and how they might look to the public are likely to delay the time when firms will be ready to make their audits public. Furthermore, as we shall see, the data tend to be pretty slippery—and subject to a variety of interpretations and misinterpretations.

The exceptional example of Abt Associates' intention to make its audit was noted above. This audit is reported in the 1971 combined financial and social audit. The "Abt Associates, Inc. Social Audit" consists of a Social Balance Sheet and a Social Income Statement, which are described as follows:

The social balance sheet presents the social net assets to date, expressed as "Society's Equity" in the social resources of the Company. The social income statement represents the net social income provided by company operations to staff, community, general public, and clients.

31

The major social asset listed is the staff which is measured at the discounted present value of the payroll weighted by the average expected future tenure of Abt staff members, corrected for training investment less "accumulated training obsolescence." This accounts for over $9 million of the company's estimated "Total Social Assets Available" of almost $12 million.

Among the "Social Commitments" on the balance sheet are such interesting items as "Pollution from Electric Power Production" which is described in this way:

> The company consumed 56,000 KWH of electric power in 1971 and 54,000 KWH in 1970. The company recognizes an obligation to society based on the cost of abatement of air pollution created in the production of this power. This cost is estimated at $.02 per KWH.

The issue of employment practice shows up in the Social Income Statement under "Social Costs to Staff" in the form of $3600 which the company estimated as underpayment to minority group members or women in 1970. The statement indicates that these inequities were eliminated in 1971.

Social benefits to staff consist of conventional employee benefits plus "Career Advancement." Costs to staff, in addition to inequality of opportunity mentioned above, consists of layoffs and terminations plus a large amount of overtime worked but not paid. Social costs and benefits to the community and the general public consist generally of services consumed and taxes paid.

In all honesty, we do not feel that we have been able to digest fully the meaning of this diligent and innovative effort. It is quite unlike any other efforts at social auditing in format, and particularly in its aspiration to express all issues in dollar terms. It does *not*, insofar as we can see, offer a significant tool for improving the firm's profitability although, as we have noted, some activities were, in fact, improved.

It should be noted that Abt Associates is a small company, manned by top officials of a like mind both on social audits and on the issues with which the audit was concerned; that they were aware of the profile which would emerge; that the range of issues on which they reported was distinctive of the type of business they are in, and that they selected the yardsticks and methodology themselves. It was likely that even in the areas in which their performance would not look "good," the fact that the firm was concerned with problems that seem to be built into their way of doing business would portray them as foresighted.

The scope of the audits varies greatly. For example, several firms' criteria tend to focus on one of several constitutencies about which a firm may be concerned: its employees. Others express interest in how they are serving their several constituencies, for example, employees, clients, and the community at large. In practice, a couple of firms are initially concentrating on internal matters, one because they decided that was the area of greatest initial payoff, the other because the employee panels which they convened chose to concentrate there. There are indications that a third company will concentrate a good deal of its effort internally. It turns out that internal performance is easier to measure largely because the data are more readily available.

At least one company, however, is already covering a wide spectrum that ranges over: employment and training; pollution; serving the consumer's needs and providing product safety; contributions and social programs. In addition, it found itself confronted by the fact that some of its associated retailers were involved with pornography, and that a large amount of its profit came from the sale of cigarettes. Thus it found itself embroiled in questions of how the goods and services it produces match the needs of society—in short, of how its basic business affects the community, not just the usefulness of its so-called "social programs." A bank, in addition to examining the status of minority and female employees, is looking at its efforts to develop minority business and middle- and low-income housing.

There is as much variety of methods as there is of content. In one instance, panels of employees (blacks, women, young professionals, old-time professionals, and so on) were assembled and the broad topic of the social issues which the company confronted vis-à-vis its constituencies was presented for discussion. As indicated above, the employees focused inward. Consequently a questionnaire is being prepared based on these discussions, and the plan is to survey the employees as a whole. However, it is interesting to note, in connection with some of our earlier comments that this survey may never take place because of the sensitivities of some subordinate managers about the state of employee opinion in their departments. Apparently, they do not wish to have these data available to either their supervisors or their supervisees! In one company which chose to concentrate initially on its employees, first attention was paid to its package of fringe benefits because it felt that this area was least controversial and the information was easiest to gather. Appropriate data were compiled from company records, and an outside firm was called in to make an independent assessment. Certain inequities were discovered: insurance benefits were better for older employees (generally more highly salaried) than for younger employees for whom the need was greater, for example. In the course of this investigation a number of employees were interviewed. It was learned that in fact the employees had a very imperfect understanding of the benefits. As a result they plan first to communicate the existing benefits better to the employees and then possibly to modify the package to fit better what the employees say they want.

Next the question of employee safety records was addressed, but here, as we have indicated, difficulties began to appear. The next step which was envisioned was an employee morale survey, but here again this move promises to produce enough internal difficulties so that it is being contemplated with great care and may not, in fact, be undertaken. Another direction being considered is a survey of stockholders to determine their support—or lack thereof—for the company's socially responsible activities and for a possible enlargement of them. There is a difference of opinion within the executive group about the wisdom of this venture.

The company which covered and uncovered the widest range of issues seems to have done so largely through record gathering and through unstructured discussion with company personnel. Illustrative is the problem of solid waste pollution with which the company found itself involved. Since the company does business in over a thousand communities, the task of getting some "objective" measure of performance is staggering. The response has been for the official conducting the audit to talk to representatives of the company in a number of communities to collect their judgments.

Several auditors are interested in ascertaining the true, as opposed to out-of-pocket, costs of the firms' social programs. One reports success but is not revealing how this was accomplished. The others have found that their present accounting systems do not permit this. One is planning to change its accounting to make this possible by breaking out data in new categories.

Another potentially interesting development lies in the intention of one auditor to compare the decision processes and criteria of managers of social programs. A management team has been assembled to do a social audit. Those members of the team who are responsible for social programs have been asked to "map" their area of responsibility, to spell out their objectives, and the rationale for their actions.

To the extent that it is possible to generalize, then, we can say that the company-sponsored social audits that are now underway vary so greatly as to make the term itself extremely elastic; are modest and exploratory; use a variety of yardsticks; and employ methods which are relatively straightforward and undemanding.

There is a considerable tendency to focus on the status of employees. This, of course, is an area of long established concern and is novel insomuch as it is now considered as part of a broader "audit." We sense another difference from the past in that the present concern over employee status has a stronger tone that the firm owes the employees decent and pleasant work conditions and fulfilling work.

Audits by Investors[8]

In its registration statement, The Dreyfus Third Century Fund, Inc. described its purpose as "investment in portfolio companies which, in the opinion of Management, have demonstrated concern for improving the quality of life in America."[9] It described the following areas of "the quality of life in America" as relevant:

Protection and improvement of the environment and the proper use of the nation's natural resources, consumer and occupational safety, product purity and its effect on the environment, equal employment opportunity, the health, education and housing demands of America or in other areas which help to improve the quality of life in the United States.

This statement was followed by the acknowledgement "that there are few accepted standards in this area of the Fund's objectives. . . ."

By the spring of 1972, The Third Century Fund had selected 20 industries for analysis on the basis of, in the words of one of its officers, "time available, probability of investment, and what we can learn by looking at that industry." The companies in these industries were being studied by a team of 6 analysts who were collecting data directly from the companies via interviews with company personnel.

One infers that the long-standing relationship of the several funds of the parent Dreyfus Corporation to such companies coupled with

[8] One source (The Corporate Information Center) reported that, as of February 1972, there were 14 mutual funds devoted to socially responsible investment. We have concentrated on the two that were most visible at the end of 1971.
[9] Registration Statement Form S5, The Dreyfus Third Century Fund, Inc., filed with the Securities and Exchange Commission on May 7, 1971.

35

the obvious fact that it is in their economic self-interest to get on the "good list," gives the Third Century Fund leverage on getting cooperation from such companies beyond that available to most outside auditors. The evidence is that Third Century is, in fact, more successful than most in their endeavors. It should be noted, for example, that in the area of minority employment the Third Century Fund asks for—and often receives—the company's "EEO-1" report which is filed with the Equal Employment Opportunities Commission. This report is ordinarily not available to the public; the Commission reports its findings periodically but only on an aggregated industry basis.

While the initial list of issues affecting the quality of life was quite long and open-ended, the Fund is concentrating in its initial cut on 4 areas: equality of employment opportunity, ecology, product purity and safety, and occupational health and safety. Because of the competitive position of the Fund, its precise methods are confidential. However, it is developing what it regards as a fairly complex weighting scheme together with a computer program for evaluating companies. Each company will be compared on a relative basis within its own industry, a standard of comparison that other "auditors" have also come to.

A novel and interesting aspect of the Fund's auditing is that they are paying attention to the corporation's procedures for reviewing the performance of the head of each operating division. A review which judges him solely on financial contribution does not pass their muster; his performance in areas of social concerns must also be considered.

Certain decisions that the Fund's officers have made are of interest. For instance, mere hiring of minority group members is only one aspect of a company's performance that is examined. What is of special interest is whether or not they are bringing minority group members into management. Good labor relations are not considered since it is assumed that this is an accepted standard of performance for modern firms. Corporate contributions are rated of low importance since "what a company does inside is more important than its charity." More controversial issues such as investment in South Africa are being passed over for the moment.

In its "Preliminary Prospectus" the Social Dimensions Fund, Inc., another such effort, stated its "dual objective" as:

. . . to seek capital appreciation while limiting investments to those companies which are responding to the changing *social dimensions* of

36

the times. A company may exhibit its response to these *social dimensions* through its products or services, its marketing methods or its manner of conducting its daily corporate life.

Under the heading "Research Policies," the prospectus announced that the Fund "has entered into an agreement with the Council on Economic Priorities" to "produce information relating to the behavior of corporations and industries on matters of social responsibility." It described the Council as "presently concentrating on four major areas: minority and employment [sic], impact on the environment, defense and military production and foreign investment."

This statement is an accurate reflection of the Council's concerns. However, this listing of issue areas does not correspond exactly to those mentioned by Mr. Ralph Quintar, President of the Social Dimensions Fund, when we interviewed him in November 1971. At that time he mentioned his concern with the following dimensions of social performance: consumerism—covering perhaps a half-dozen areas such as nutrition, labeling, packaging, and so on; minority employment, training, and advancement; minority relations such as deposits in black banks, a black on the board, black dealers and suppliers, or sponsorship of a Mesbic program in minority entrepreneurship; community involvement in the form of making grants or loaning people to community programs; pollution control; employee safety and other working conditions; employee benefits; and corporate giving. He placed little emphasis on the then popular issue of investment in South Africa, and did not mention defense contracting.

With a staff somewhat smaller than that of the Third Century Fund, Mr. Quintar is building a data bank on the *Fortune* 500. This data bank will produce "a social summary of a corporation." Mr. Quintar thinks "the profile will always be qualitative"—a contrast to the Dreyfus computerized weighting scheme. His methods are more eclectic than those of the Dreyfus group. In addition to his Fund's affiliation with the Council on Economic Priorities, he has also developed a network of knowledgeable informants on the social performance of business and industry. Finally, he, too, is going directly to the companies for information, most particularly on minority policies. He, too, seeks out the EEO-1 report. Unlike Dreyfus, however, he is not having a great deal of success in this effort.

In his priority of values, minority hiring, training, and advancement take first place. On other social issues (pollution, for example) circumstances vary widely from industry to industry, he feels, that the minority issue, which cuts across industries evenly, is the single yardstick that should enjoy a veto power. (One might want to adjust this judgment by region.)

While the two funds, with essentially the same objectives, have differences in their operations, both have come rather firmly to two quite interesting conclusions. The first is that the quality of a company's social performance tends to be uniform across the board. Representatives of both funds affirm that they do not find anomalies of a firm performing well on one or more dimensions but poorly on others—at least for the dimensions they have chosen. This conclusion, we shall see, will not hold up as the range of criteria is extended.

More surprising, the representatives of both funds strongly reject the notion that there is a trade-off between social responsibility and profitability—again, at least as they define social responsibility. This is contrary to the public view of the funds as portrayed in the press as offering the socially responsible investor who is willing to forego some profits a place to put his money.

However, it would appear that in the course of their investigations the officers of both funds are finding that socially responsible companies are also more profitable than average. Supporting evidence in at least one area comes from an analysis done by Joseph Bragdon of H. C. Wainwright and Co., and Professor John Marlin of N.Y.U. [1972]. Using the data of the Council on Economic Priorities on pollution in the paper industries, Bragdon and Marlin established a strong correlation between good environmental performance according to paper industry standards and profit performance.

The officers of both funds have come to the conclusion that the socially responsible company tends to be one with management whose competence is across the board. As one man put it: "Smart is smart is smart." It should be pointed out that neither fund believes that social responsibility is such a perfect predictor of performance that it should be made the basis for the final investment decision. In the case of both firms, getting good marks on social responsibility merely puts a company on the list of eligibles from which later investment decisions will be made in terms of the financial attractiveness of the various firms on the eligible list. Nevertheless, both are optimistic about the investment potential of the lists which they are preparing. Both deny that they will be marketing to prospective investors who are willing to give up profits in order to be socially responsible.

Some light is thrown on this conclusion by the fact that both firms have excluded investment in such countries as South Africa as one of their criteria of social responsibility. When this criterion was applied to the portfolio of Princeton University, it was found that exclusion of companies doing business in South Africa would lower the rate of return of the portfolio by 3 per cent [Malkiel and Quandt, 1971]. Companies that would have been eliminated included Polaroid, IBM, and Xerox which, by other criteria, have a reputation for being socially responsible. Clearly the answer one gets can depend on the criteria he uses.

This issue of the relationship of social responsibility—and of what types—to quality of management and financial performance is one that obviously needs further exploration.

Public Interest Auditors

The Corporate Information Center of the National Council of Churches is one of the public interest organizations that have sprung up recently. For two years before its founding there was a committee whose purpose was to accumulate and disseminate information on corporate responsibility in five areas: the environment; consumer health, welfare and safety; foreign investment; military procurement and production; minorities and women.

The Center sees its role not so much in gathering original data on corporations but in synthesizing the work done by others in individual areas of social concern. An example of its activities is its October 1971 volume, *Corporate Responsibility and Religious Institutions*. This is a collection of papers on social responsibility, together with an extensive bibliography and list of people and institutions concerned with the topic. It will have access to a data bank that is being compiled to provide computerized retrieval of literature on the environment, urban and public affairs, and consumer affairs. They have, however, made some original attempts at data gathering, having surveyed some 60 companies in church investment portfolios. They have received about a 50 per cent return.

Though churches may choose not to invest in corporations that are using policies of which they do not approve, the Center does not believe this is a very effective instrument for changing corporate behavior because of the relatively small size of church investments.

Rather, the Center proposes to use moral suasion by getting the churches and affiliated groups to try to influence corporations directly, and by influencing the investment policies of larger investors such as the foundations, mutual funds, and the investment community at large—at least a scattering of which are displaying interest in "socially responsible investment." In addition, they are well aware of the impact of public bad-mouthing, as we have noted in the first chapter.

During 1971, the press gave a good deal of attention to another public interest auditor, The Council on Economic Priorities. The Council was founded by Alice Tepper (now Alice Tepper Marlin) and dates back to the time when Miss Tepper, working as an investment analyst three years out of college, was approached by one of the firm's accounts, a synagogue, which asked her to put together a peace portfolio. While its original intention was to provide data for the guidance of investors, the Council seems to have had its main impact via the media, and the consequent use of their findings by groups attempting to influence corporations directly.

The areas of concern for the Council are: minority hiring and training, and help to the minority community; the environment; military contracting; impact of corporations on countries abroad; and the political area (where they have not as yet done any work). The Council is deliberately not considering such issues as consumerism and job safety which it believes are being handled adequately by others.

The most prominent products of the Council to date are its journal, "Economic Priorities Report" which appears every two months, a book *Efficiency in Death* [1970], and its monographic publication *Paper Profits*, a detailed study of pollution in the paper industry on a company-by-company and plant-by-plant basis. In process at the end of 1971 were studies of pollution in the steel industry and in utilities, minority group practices in banks, and a *Guide to Corporations*, evaluating 45 corporations across the board. The council regards the latter effort, though helpful, relatively superficial compared to the rigorous standards they have established for their industry pollution studies.

Methods of data collection vary by area. Military contracting, for example, is studied by plowing laboriously through Pentagon documents. In their major fields of interest—minority problems and the environment—data are gathered directly from companies via questionnaires administered to those closest to the problem. In the case of environmental pollution technical people are utilized;

the head of urban and public affairs and of the EEO program is consulted on minority policies. These questionnaire findings are supplemented with other *ad hoc* sources of information. For example, in the case of minority employment, black "headhunters" are consulted on the reputations of firms, and the EEO-1 report, where available, is analyzed.

In the instance of environmental pollution, where the Council has made its major effort, it is proudest of its methods. According to officers of the Council they begin by consulting the best Federal, state, and corporate sources as well as independent technical experts on the state of the art of pollution control specific to the industry to be studied. On the basis of this technical information, very detailed questionnaires are prepared for administration to appropriate company personnel. In addition, extensive interviews are conducted.

One may wonder, considering the reluctance of companies doing their own audits to make their findings public, how warmly firms welcome such public interest inquiries. The answer is, imperfectly. However, the Council reports that cooperation is improving, particularly as the press calls attention to companies who are reluctant to assist. The irony of cooperativeness in the paper industry is that it did not correlate with the Council's rating of companies' performance. Many companies in the industry simply did not know where they stood relative to their competitors.

As with other auditors, the Council recognizes that problems and issues of social responsibility are industry specific, and it emphasizes that it is attempting to locate the good guys as well as the bad guys within each industry.

The Council has established a goal of updating its studies on a yearly basis. Considering the number of industries the Council might consider, and the number of issues with which it is concerned, one must question the workload it is cutting out for itself, as well as the applicability of the criteria it is using in all the areas of concern. At present it is operating on somewhat tenuous financing, relying on the services of highly dedicated young people who are willing to work for less than their talents would net for them elsewhere.

Finally, we turn to the relationship of the Council's work to the finding of the two mutual funds that social responsibility is a rather homogeneous phenomenon. The Council's preliminary findings indicate that, on the issues of minority and pollution policies, companies tend to perform either well or poorly on both. But these

41

issues, they believe, have little relationship to performance on more ideological topics such as military contracting. One would expect the same lack of correlation with investment in countries such as South Africa. Clearly there appear to be two separate packages of issues of social concern involved in the judgments being made of American corporations, and the packages bear little or no relationship to each other.

Summary

As heterogeneous and partial as these findings may be, they do testify to the fact that programmatic proposals for social auditing of business firms have resulted or been paralleled by some attempts to give substance to the notion. In most cases these must be regarded as attempts in process. Some might fail; others might produce some surprising results. Probably the Council on Economic Priorities, of the institutions we have covered, has produced the most concrete outputs, but it is held together by the extraordinary dedication of its members and by slender financing.

The variety of criteria and approaches which have been applied do not stem from some sort of pluralistic ignorance. Persons who are doing things differently are often in close communication with each other, and sometimes the same individual has done different things in different situations. The variations seem to come from differences in personal preference and style as well as from attempts to adapt to the needs and resources of specific situations. The result is that we are confronted with a variety of versions of what a social audit can be, how it can be done, and for what purposes. All this reflects the fact that, as a society, we do not yet have a generally accepted set of definitions of just what constitutes social responsibility. These experiences thus provide the potential for learning about and understanding what may be a new social institution in its inception.

Considering the *ad hoc* way in which these several efforts have evolved, one must assume that they do not give us a full scheme of what a social audit may be. And, considering their pioneering nature, one must further assume that they do not touch on the full range of conceptual and methodological problems that will evolve. We shall try to anticipate what these potentials may be in the next chapter.

The Future of Corporate Social Audits

In this section we speculate on what form or forms the concept of corporate social audits may take in the future. Our goal is not to prescribe or predict a single form of audit. This is premature. We assume that if the concept has a future, its form or forms will evolve largely out of the experience of people and institutions in doing audits, out of reactions of others to those audits, and out of the mores of the community as the audits develop.

We should note that some experienced and wise observers raise grave doubts that this kind of auditing is possible at all. In their view, we do not yet have either the language or the tools to do it, at least as it is currently being discussed. In a degree, this chapter is an exploration of that very question.

The discussion will be organized around the uses to which an audit might be put, the information needs implied by those uses, and the problems involved in getting and using such information. In the course of this exploration it will become evident that there are many types of general knowledge about auditing, social responsibility, and the behavior and thinking of executives that we need to have in order to understand the full implications of social auditing. We shall not try to be comprehensive because comprehensiveness would imply at least that one knew the boundaries of the problem and, as we observe the experience of others and contemplate the problems involved in social auditing, the boundaries keep expanding and their locations keep changing.

Regardless of who does them, audits may have three basic consequences: to influence decision making and actions within the firm; to influence investment decisions; and to inform the public, who in turn may either attempt to influence investment decisions or to influence corporate behavior through government action or in other ways.

As we have already seen, audits may be and are being undertaken by three different types of entities: businesses auditing themselves, investors auditing businesses, and public interest groups auditing businesses. While the three different entities have different interests and viewpoints, almost all of the problems and possibilities of social audits are revealed when one considers the possibilities of business self-audits. Two obvious differences stand out: first, outside auditors may have difficulty getting access to information that is internal to to the firms they are auditing; second, business firms may have trouble getting credibility for what they report. While business firms may want for internal decision making some data the "outside auditors" might not be interested in, and while firms might wish to ignore some matters the outside auditors are interested in, the latter have the capacity to encourage firms to pay attention to these matters. Hence, a fully extended internal audit for the firm ought to be at least as extensive as an outside audit (noting, of course, the internal difficulties we mentioned earlier). In addition, as we shall immediately demonstrate, it is clearly in the interest of a corporation to undertake such a self-audit. Accordingly, we will simplify matters by concentrating on business self-audits, and treat investor and public interest audits residually as is necessary.

To start with, the various potential users will find different uses for the different types of audits a corporation might undertake. Audits conducted by corporations and kept private will presumably be designed specially for internal decision making and, to the extent that they are kept private, will be of no use to investors or social critics. Furthermore, they will correspond to the values of corporate leadership. Those audits done by the corporation for public reporting will presumably be designed to mesh with the definitions of social responsibility held by the investing community and social critics. (Since social critics probably will be continuously raising new issues, there will be some lag in public corporate social reporting.) These two groups, of course, will often disagree with each other, and with the corporate leadership. Corporate auditors, for example, and investors *may* dispute the relevance of some issues raised by social critics—say, doing business with South Africa. Thus corporate-conducted audits intended for public reporting may not, probably would not, contain all the information that the corporation would want for internal decision making. Hence, taken alone, they would be somewhat weak for the latter purpose. By the same token, those conducted for internal decision-making may not contain all that the critics and/or investors might want, or in the way they might want it.

Investor-conducted audits will by definition be tailored to suit the needs of the investment community. Since the social critics are likely to be concerned with a wider and shifting range of issues than the investment community might consider, investor audits may not serve the entire range of interests of the social critics. Investor audits, assuming they are made public, may reach the corporation a little late—after the corporation has been judged on the first round. And they may miss items in which the company is interested.

Audits carried out by public interest groups would in turn be designed to fill their needs. Since they are likely to cover at least as wide a range of issues as the investors are interested in, they are likely to serve the purposes of this latter group. This pattern might break down, however, if corporate or investor audits are well developed and the public interest groups decide to concentrate their attention on new issues or selectively attend to special issues on which they would raise higher standards than would the other groups. In addition, there is almost inevitably an element of "crusading" in such endeavors which may taint their credibility for the investor, the corporate management, or both. Finally, public interest audits, like investor audits, will probably reach the corporation late—after the corporation has been judged.

The above pattern suggests at least one thing: corporations have an interest in making their own audits before they are audited by others—a not too surprising conclusion. (We should observe here that the very fact they audit themselves is a real plus in terms of a firm's relations with social pressure groups; such corporate self-scrutiny, if done honestly, is a prime objective of their efforts.)

Business Self-Audits

Business self-audits may be done either to inform investors and the general public of the social performance of the firm or to guide the actions of the firm. While the information needs for these two broad purposes overlap considerably, there are, as we shall see, circumstances under which they may vary. At least some versions of what an audit might require in the way of information for guidance of internal corporate decisions would present broader demands than would audits for public consumption. Conversely, in some respects the information demands for public reporting will be more exacting. Because audits for internal reasons are likely to precede public audits in time, we will consider them first.

A word should be said about what may be perceived in the tone of the passages which follow. Without our intending it, they may sound negative, and thus align us with those who say "it can't be done." If so, the reader has misread us. It is true we devote a good deal of attention to the difficulties of doing many things. This is simply because our strategy is to explore the logical idealized extension that might be implied by different versions of a corporate social audit. It is not often in this world that we attain the ideal. But the ideal is often worth exploring because it helps us be wiser in the compromises we adopt. And, since in our judgment there are some useful steps that can now be taken within the state of the art, we would urge the reader to be patient.

Another circumstance that contributes to the tone of the passages that follow is the fact that we have been diligent in pursuing implications beyond those that are immediately obvious.

In the early stages of the development of a concept such as the corporate social audit one moves from rather abstract programmatic statements to the grubby problem of making them operational. We are content neither with those who say blithely that "it must be done so it can be done," and stop there; nor with those who would limit the discussion to the problems of measuring and evaluating organizations, or the willingness or unwillingness of the people involved to do so. The worlds of programmatic statements and of practical operations are quite different, involving real and complex difficulties.

Further, the early stages of a developing concept are different than the later. What is foggy today may seem misty tomorrow, and clear on the day after, and vice versa. We are, then, seeking to push the investigation beyond the concept to the implementation and, hopefully, work our way through the fog at least to the mist.

AUDITING FOR INTERNAL DECISIONS.　As we have noted, the logic of the social audit in its most elaborate form is exposed when we look at it from the point of view of corporate internal decision making. Here we can identify four (potential) reasons for doing audits that any given person may have in any combination. In increasing order of their difficulty, they are: to satisfy the conscience of corporate officers; to anticipate and avoid community (including employee, stockholder, and government) pressure; to solve social problems; to increase long-range profits. Let us look at each one in turn.

Satisfying the Corporate Conscience   While satisfying his own conscience may not be the sole motive for an executive wanting a social audit, it is bound to be a component of any man's thinking on this issue. The basic question he asks is whether he can justify his and his firm's performance in terms of his own self-image? Or, if he anticipates answering to the public, he will ask (probably implicitly) what sort of information he needs in order to feel comfortable defending the actions of his firm. An audit designed to serve this need focuses on the level of effort. "Are we doing all that can reasonably be expected of us?" Even though he may be subject to criticism, he should be able to justify the existing state of affairs to himself and others.

An audit for a businessman who wants to satisfy himself and his definition of the corporate conscience will consist of an inventory of what he is doing, of what others are doing, of what the law requires, and of what has been proposed as possible. It is then up to him to make up his mind. (Things get stickier if he begins to ask whether or not his programs are effective, and whether they meet the real needs of the community. We would argue that when he does that he is going beyond trying to satisfy his own conscience. We will take that up later.)

An inventory of what the firm is doing may or may not be readily available. In large complex firms, socially relevant activities may be widely dispersed and it may be necessary to make an internal survey in order to assemble information for executive consideration. This could present difficulties. We will not know for sure until a few fairly large and complex firms report their experiences on this matter, but our strong suspicion, from what we have seen thus far, is that the internal survey will be very complicated in terms of both definition and data collection. Such knowledge, which to an outsider seems easy to attain, frequently is difficult to trace as we have mentioned earlier. For example, a firm with plants in a hundred or more communities will have a considerable task enumerating all the community activities of its executives.

A problem may lie in deciding where to draw the line on what to consider as "socially relevant." An individual businessman, for example, may be sensitive to the possibility of sharp marketing practices, poor product safety and the like, but not as interested in minority matters. In our construct of the purpose of the audit we are here describing, this is exactly where a man's own conscience comes in.

The yardsticks, then, are determined by the auditor's own value system. But assessing "level of effort" may be quite another matter. One route is to look at the dollar cost of the firm's socially responsible actions. We have already seen the difficulties the Bank of America has reported in this regard. While out-of-pocket costs may be readily available, arriving at the "true costs" is likely to be much more difficult. What amount of executive time has gone into the administration of the programs? Should a portion of the top executives' time spent on thinking about the dealing with social responsibility be allocated? Should the "opportunity costs"—the return on this money that might have been realized invested in the firm's regular business—be considered? It is obvious that any attempt to assess true costs will result in a range of estimates, each justifiable by some reasonable rationale. Probably the wisest course of action is to have the firm's accountants present the full range of costs for the corporate officers to consider until the officers decide which is most useful and viable—or, perhaps, which one simply satisfices.

Here we need some developmental work by the accounting profession and their kin to instruct us as to what is possible and desirable, and so that outside "auditors" to whom the data might be reported would know the meaning of the several arbitrary conventions that may emerge.

Knowing what he is doing in terms of activities and funds committed, the businessman must then make his own evaluation of whether or not he is satisfied. This will be largely affected by his knowledge of what others are doing, what he thinks is possible, what he believes is acceptable, his own goals, and what is required of him. There are data on corporate giving, frequently broken down by industry, though the reporting of them will prove unsatisfactory in many ways for comparative purposes. There are the "grapevine" reports within a particular community which can and do serve as guidelines. On minority and female employment, there is the EEOC's aggregate reporting; on pollution, the Council on Economic Priorities is developing norms on pollution control for *some* industries. There are laws for product and employee safety, and so on. There are records of court and administrative agency actions on many business practices. In some instances there are norms for industry performance on employee safety. However, such knowledge is likely to be unevenly available on all the issues for which an executive may want to judge his behavior.

Further, if a particular top manager wants to include such currently attractive concepts as "quality of life within the firm," he will find that comparative measurements will be very difficult. As part of the development of the technology of social audits we need a review of the norms presently available against which to judge social performance. The possibility of developing new appropriate norms should be explored where relevant.

In judging his level of effort, the top manager is likely to test that evaluation by some conception of what the business can "afford." Will this be what he is accustomed to? What others spend? What he thinks he can justify to the stockholders? What will appear acceptable to the community? What he feels "in his heart is right"? Or is it some "rational" economic cost of the effect of these expenditures on the growth of the firm? It is probably not the last of these.

Generally speaking, the problems of making an audit for purposes of satisfying the corporate social conscience are not so difficult if one does not set too high a level of aspiration, is willing to exercise judgment freely, and is content with rough data in many areas. The key to this type of audit is that the executive—or the top management group—be satisfied that he is living up to his own self-image. If this is his major concern he will probably be willing to live with imprecise cost and other data and accept the unevenness of the quality of the norms by which he judges the corporation's behavior. The uncertainties associated with this evaluation are no greater than those involved in most of the regular business decisions he has to make.

This is the least demanding type of corporate social audit. The criterion of success is whether or not the executive (and his associates) is (are) satisfied in their own mind(s). *Logically,* this type of audit could be anything from a contemplative reassessment of what he already knows, through extended discussion with his fellow executives, through the more extended type of activity we have indicated here, to a massively ambitious attempt. Since it is his own conscience or sense of ease that determines whether the executive feels he can defend his firm's behavior, it should also determine how extensive the information has to be to make this judgment. The size of the job is proportionate to the size of the conscience.

One might object that minimal efforts such as some of those suggested above scarcely qualify as an audit. We introduced them to underscore the point that there is no presently fixed notion of what a social audit is and, if the adequacy of an audit is to be judged by whether or not it served its purpose, then navel gazing cannot *per se* be ruled out. This, in turn, underscores the further point that the question of whether a social audit is "possible" is now unanswerable because the term is still so undefined. We have described here a version of an audit that at a minimal level is clearly attainable. We will later describe some versions that we deem unattainable.

However, we assume that a pure case of the above will seldom exist. What a man expects of himself will be largely conditioned by what others expect of him and by the temper of the times in which he lives. "Even judges and Congressmen and regulators are caught up in today's American Revolution," said one top government official recently. Furthermore few men will be satisfied to be "trying hard" without wanting some assurance that they are actually accomplishing something. While satisfying the conscience may be a component of every executive's motivation, it is unlikely to exist in isolation.

Anticipating and Avoiding Pressure   Firms whose motive is simply to stay out of trouble should be taken lightly *only* if this is their sole purpose. After all, Ralph Nader's main objective, laid out explicitly in *Unsafe at Any Speed*, is to make corporations responsive. One can hardly attack them for "doing things just to stay out of trouble," if responsiveness is the ultimate objective, because that is *precisely* the characteristic they are displaying: responding to community demands and pressures. Even the most socially conscious of firms ought to exhibit this concern. Experience shows that there is no necessarily perfect fit between the most well intentioned of corporate actions and the expectations of other interested and affected parties. This is particularly true in an era in which the expectations of corporate responsibility are in a constant state of change.

The reader may well ask how these concerns fit into the concept of a corporate social audit. The answer lies in the notion of matching what one is doing with what is expected of him. Clearly this is one relevant criterion—some would even say the most valid—for evaluating a corporation's social responsibility whether for public reporting or internal decision making because it means that a company is setting its values and actions in terms of the community's needs and concerns.

To the extent that the businessman wants to anticipate and avoid pressure from the outside community, employees, stockholders, customers, and the government, he needs information beyond that needed to satisfy his conscience and a higher degree of credibility and precision in the data. An inventory of what he is doing is essential. But he also needs information on the aspirations and perceived needs of these groups, on what they expect him to do, and on what they will support him for doing or attack him for failing to do. He needs to know their ability to organize and bring effective pressure to bear on him in the face of either inaction or limited response on his part.

The sample survey can play a crucial role in supplying a big part of this information. One can survey samples of the community, employees, customers, and stockholders. This is standard practice and the technology is well known. We have reported elsewhere one activity that can serve as a partial prototype for such activities, the survey that one of us did of the reaction of various Boston publics to the Boston business community. Surveys of public and community reactions to corporations or the business community are commonplace.

To understand the changing expectations of the community at large, a firm may subscribe to one of the newer syndicated sample survey services designed for this purpose. However, when it comes to sampling the communities and employees of large multidivisional companies operating in perhaps hundreds of communities, the job may take on formidable dimensions. The problems may be entirely different across divisions and across communities, and the cost of sampling that many entities could be staggering. Perhaps one needs an intelligence system to tell him which divisions and which communities are potential sources of trouble or of high diagnostic value and which, therefore, ought to be surveyed.

Sample surveying would be an inefficient and inappropriate method of anticipating and avoiding governmental pressure. Instead, good political intelligence can identify key people who could be observed and interviewed.

While sample surveys of relevant constituencies can determine their expectancies and preferences in the aggregate, this may not be an adequate measure if one wants to anticipate and avoid pressure. Aggregate opinion is not, at least in the short range, necessarily effective opinion. Groups vary in the extent to which they can organize and bring pressure to bear, and in the extent to which particular issues are likely to mobilize action. If the executive wants to allocate his resources efficiently he will want to know which aggregate phenomena are likely to take the form of effective pressure and gain the kind of public and press attention that makes them viable. This is a matter for political and social analysis.

The man who wants to stay out of trouble will judge the fit between what he is doing and the enforceable demands that others may make of him. If the fit is good, this form of audit shows that he is doing well in this regard. If the fit is poor, he has a signal to change his behavior.

All this, incidentally, rests on the premise that the cash register is not the only ballot mechanism available and that reaction to corporative behavior can and does come from sources other than customers.

For purposes of public reporting the type of political and social analysis suggested above is not needed and in fact might be inappropriate. Certainly the public will find the match between what the company is doing and the expectations of its constituencies as one relevant basis of evaluating the company's performance. The public is less likely to be sympathetic to the idea that the company is differentially responsive in proportion to the probability that a constituent is likely to organize to bring pressure.

Just as we expected to find few pure conscience satisfiers, so do we expect to find few pure trouble avoiders. However, we have suggested here a module of a social audit which would help meet the trouble-avoiding needs of a man whose total needs are more complex. This module is a logical extension of what has generally been proposed or tried—though not a drastic extension. As we have reported, at least one of the firms presently conducting an audit is contemplating carrying out one element of our module, for example, surveying its stockholders to find the extent to which they approve of present practices and might support an extension of the company's socially responsible action. Surveys of employees have been a routine matter and are a part of several proposed and actual audits. Surveys of the general public and of particular communities to learn their opinions about business in general and about particular companies have—as we indicated—also been routine.

We have merely suggested that some comprehensive auditing of the expectations and opinions of a full range of a firm's constituencies is a potential component of a corporate social audit. Generally speaking the technology is available, though the art of political and social analysis is and will continue to be imperfect.

One can think of this environmental auditing component on many levels of complexity and adequacy. It would be easy to extend its ambitions to the point where it would be too expensive and consume too much executive time and energy to meet the sensible needs of even the largest of firms. On the other hand, one could expect to find in any organization some rudimentary form of such an early warning system, even though it may consist only of tracking stockholders' complaints to find when on a given issue they have reached some experientially judged "critical point." Surveying stockholders, if one is willing to live with the sample bias of a mailed questionnaire, is inexpensive enough to be done by even a rather small firm if it is sufficiently interested. Surveys of employees are, of course, done and may be done on an almost infinitely varying scale of cost and adequacy. Generally, the decision to survey the general public or specific communities involves the commitment to a considerable outlay. This is almost always undertaken only by very large firms, and even these studies seldom, in our knowledge, go into the detail that might be implied by the above discussion. The rank-and-file businessman is more likely to decide to rely on a general perusal of published or syndicated public opinion studies of what the public feels about and expects of business in general. (Such syndicated services are becoming more generally available.)

As for the suggestion of political and social intelligence and analysis, the range of performance to which one might aspire is again very broad, and the number of steps along the range almost infinite.

In general, whether or not this particular module of a social audit is possible depends more on the resources one is able or willing or finds prudent to commit to it than on its technical feasibility (granting the useful though limited inferences one may draw from such information). To our almost certain knowledge, not even the most gigantic of giant corporations has anything like an idealized model of what such a system may be, and this may indeed be a very wise judgment. But, as we have indicated, an infinite variety of versions is possible.

Solving Social Problems   We assume that the most frequent answer we would get if we asked businessmen why they might want to conduct a social audit of their firms is that they want to understand (and/or communicate) what they are doing to contribute to the solution of society's problems. Here we would like to explore what the full information needs of such an audit might entail. Again, we will go to extremes to see what the logical extension of the position might be, and then see what fallbacks are available. We will go to a further extreme and assume that a man has adopted a policy, which some had advocated, of maximizing social contribution while setting some minimal profit level as a constraint (rather than attempting to maximize profits).

The difference between a man who wants to satisfy his conscience and the man who wants to solve social problems is not clear-cut. The two types blend into each other. The difference lies in the relative emphasis that is placed on intending to do good as compared to assuming the responsibility for doing good. The pure conscience satisfyer will be content to do what are conventionally considered to be "good things" or those that strike his particular set of values. His information needs do not extend to knowing the consequences of his actions, nor do they require an analysis of the actual needs of the society to which he is being ostensibly responsible. To the extent that he assumes responsibility for the consequences of his actions and for meeting the needs of the society, his information needs proliferate, probably beyond the state of the art and beyond practical feasibility, and the judgments he must make become increasingly difficult if not impossible.

To the extent that a man took literally the notion that he wanted to turn his business to the solution of social problems, he would need an inventory of the resources he can bring to bear on the problems. Implicit is the notion that he would also know *how*[10] those resources could be brought to bear to solve those problems, and the conviction that his resources *can* solve them. His judgment of how well he is presently doing would be based on the *effects* of his present programs as they were matched against what he might achieve via some "optimum" matching of his resources to the society's needs and priorities. Presumably this judgment would be made in the context of some trade-off between social programs and his regular business such that the latter should be sufficiently profitable to remain in business. At any time, a firm will have the option of considering new social programs. The probability of success with such programs will have to be based on judgment. This

[10] The proposed ways of remedying many social problems are varied and usually based on an imperfect knowledge of the social processes involved. Any of the decisions we are talking about would depend on the businessman's explicit or implicit model of these processes.

judgment will be aided by good diagnosis of the problem, assessment of the firm's resources, and—where relevant—other firm experience with similar programs.

It is unlikely that anyone would or could undertake the full job of data gathering, analysis, and judgments implied by the above formulation. However, any attempt deliberately to solve social problems implies some evaluation of this sort. The "optimizing" procedures described above can be approximated in varying degrees.

A key consideration will be the measurement and assessment of effects of existing programs. Socially responsible corporate actions vary in their amenability to measurement and the degree to which there is agreement on the criteria whereby they are to be judged.

Pollution control can be measured in terms of the level of effluence which is emitted. There is less agreement, however, on proper performance levels or on the relative importance of different types of effluence. To the extent that performance levels are legislated, this ambiguity is eliminated. If the level is or is not legislated, is the judgment to be made in absolute terms (zero pollution), in terms of "acceptable" levels (what can we get away with? are we conforming to the law?), in terms of economic feasibility, in terms of industry performance? And how do you handle the trade-offs? If rigid standards mean higher costs to the point where products are out of the reach of the disadvantaged, is this a social good?

When one turns to employment policies, the problem appears again. The regularly accepted measures are not unambiguous or at least their assessment is not. The "success" of a program for training the hard-core unemployed can be measured in terms of numbers completing the course, being hired, and being retained in the job. These measures will be more complete to the extent that they can be compared with the success of similar programs on similar populations (a difficult set of comparisons to run, incidentally). However, if the program is judged in terms of the extent to which it "solved" or contributed to the solution of a social problem the verdict may be dismal. Any one company's contribution is likely to affect a miniscule dimension of the problem unless it is a very large company in a small community; and the second-order consequences of its programs are usually highly unpredictable. For example, are they simply "creaming" the minority community and enabling (encouraging?) its leadership to move out either physically or psychologically, leaving behind only destructive models for the young to emulate? Some observers say so.

There are complications in evaluating minority advancement

within an organization. This is perhaps best illustrated by a recent judgment of the Civil Rights Commission that the Federal government discriminates against blacks in the upper ranks of the civil service. It develops that a majority of the civil servants in those ranks are members of such professions as law, medicine, and economics. Is the fault that of the Federal government or that of the professions which failed to recruit blacks to their ranks? To what extent is the business firm responsible for the extent to which the educational system has failed the black community? To what extent can it be expected to do something about it? And, on another dimension, is it a "social good" to give its customers poorer service or products (including its disadvantaged customers) as a result of compensating for society's past failures?

But these are the easy ones: other social programs are much more difficult to measure and assess. Xerox has released a substantial number of employees to work full time on social programs. The input, the cost in salaries, and foregone opportunities for the company, may be measureable. But, even if the performance of the programs can be and is evaluated, can the contribution of the Xerox employee be isolated from all of the other factors that contributed to the program's performance? One convention might be to allocate to the Xerox company that proportion of the performance that represents the ratio of Xerox's dollar contribution to the total budget of the program. This makes the questionable assumption that the man's performance on a social program is proportionate to his value to Xerox in his regular job. The matter would be different if Xerox had contributed his salary to the program. Then, since a Xerox dollar is like any other dollar, Xerox's contribution to the social benefits of the program would be proportionate to its share of the total budget.

Corporate contributions—financial and other—can ordinarily be measured only in terms of such intermediate effects as number of people who received a given type of service. Few social programs can document what the delivery of their programs did for the people they benefit, never mind the comparative worth of other projects in which the corporation might have involved itself.

Most types of programs are not only difficult but expensive to evaluate. Educational and community development programs are regularly being evaluated by the Federal and other governments. Considering the magnitude of government investment in such programs, even imperfect evaluations are worth the cost if they can contribute to our understanding of how to implement such programs. However, it is doubtful that any given company would very often find it feasible to make an evaluation of their contribution to such a program in terms of its measurable effects.

These difficulties in measuring and assessing the ultimate consequences of corporate socially responsible actions suggest that process audits be employed in proportion to the difficulty and costs of making the measurements and assessments we have been discussing. For the businessman who wants to assess his social program, the observer would develop an analytic description of what is actually being done (there are likely to be some surprises even here) and a statement of what the best known practice is (let us say training the hard-core unemployed). The businessman will compare what he was doing against the best known practice and judge whether the comparison warrants his changing his actions.

An instance in which a process audit is very likely to be preferable to a performance audit would be in the assessment of a bank's program in support of minority businesses. To keep things simple we will confine our attention solely to the problem of judging the program's contribution to the society. A more ambitious goal might be to judge the contribution of the program to the bank's long-range profits. However, if we find the simpler task intractable, we are unlikely to undertake the more difficult one.

To begin with, an estimate of the bank's contribution to the success of the minority businesses which its program supported would have to be made in the context of an estimate of the probability of success of those businesses in the absence of any action from the bank. This estimate would have to include a further estimate of the probability of similar action by another bank in the absence of its own action. Such a basis for judgment of the bank's contribution is conceivable if it were possible to develop norms for reasonably comparable businesses not in the bank's program. But, at best, the development of such norms would be difficult and expensive and, as we see, would be only one element in the audit assessment.

Next, a decision that the program had helped any given business, and to what extent, could be made only after some reasonable time had elapsed, since an infusion of money and other assistance is virtually guaranteed to sustain the life of any business over the short haul.

One would, of course, want to know the true costs of the program. This would involve the costs of administering the program, including such technical assistance as would be given in support of the loans. Additionally, one would need to know the "opportunity costs," that is, the difference between the return which the bank would have received by using the money in its customary ways minus the return on the loans made via this program—assuming that the latter is less profitable than the bank's ordinary business. Since the return from loans in the minority business program would be a function of both the rate of interest charged and the rate of default, one could calculate this return with accuracy only after the program had been in existence long enough to know the default rate. Early in the program, informed judgments could be made with increasing confidence as the program began developing its track record.

Now we may turn to the task of measuring the program's social contribution. In the discussions of minority entrepeneurship, three objectives are usually cited: retention of earnings in the minority community, provision of jobs for minority group members, and—less often mentioned, but conceivably most important—contribution to the development of a viable social structure in the minority community. It is also arguable that if the business is a service or retail business, as many minority enterprises are, it will serve the community better either by giving its patrons better goods and services or by lowering prices. This would constitute a fourth objective. There is a considerable body of literature on the feasibility of these objectives, particularly of the first two. A best judgment is that the first two objectives, though possible and desirable, would under the most optimistic conditions contribute only a small bit to the needs for money and jobs in the minority community.[11] Hence the third and fourth objectives must be given serious consideration.

The retention of earnings in the minority community can be calculated initially by noting the profits earned by the firms in the program. However, since these profits are earned presumably in competition with other business firms, at least an informed judgment must be made as to where these profits were deflected from and/or if there is any social cost in this deflection of profits.

The number of jobs created may seem to be a straightforward matter. But a simple tabulation of the number of persons employed by minority enterprises does not answer the question completely unless it considers the number of minority group members who would have been hired by nonminority businesses under

[11] Dr. Andrew Brimmer of the Federal Reserve Board has written widely to this point.

alternate circumstances (for example, if a chain store in the ghetto were owned by whites rather than blacks). One might want to make some adjustment for some gain in morale that blacks might experience by working for a black employer.

Apropos improvements in the social structure of minority communities, there is no obvious and easy way to measure such a phenomenon, though various behavioral science concepts, measures, and techniques could be brought to bear on the task.[12]

But, improvement in social structure is an intermediate benefit, which is relevant only if it results in an increased ability of the members of the community to help each other, provide role models for young people growing up in the community, reduce social pathologies, and the like. Data on many such matters are often available, but with such data in hand one would have to decide over what area the bank's program might have an effect (which may be possible), and then judge what portion of any improvement to allocate to any particular program. There almost certainly would be a long lead time between the inauguration of a lending program and traceable social effects in the community.

Finally, one would want to know if the firms in this program have produced a better or poorer product or service at lower or higher prices than would have been available in their absence.

An elaborate assessment of the sort required above may be conceivable at considerable cost, ingenuity, and effort. Such an undertaking might be warranted for evaluating something as large as a federal social program. It is scarcely possible that it would be justified for a single firm's effort.

At this point the reader may either be intrigued by the complexity of the problem, irritated by our nitpicking, or both. We have gone through this exercise, however, to illustrate the vast difference between the easy verbalization "assess the true costs and the social benefits" and the actual operations that may be implied by this verbalization. If the reader thinks we have been needlessly detailed, he is invited to inspect any one of the steps we have proposed and judge whether or not the dropping of it might not lead to a misleading judgment.

[12] Indices of social health and pathology are, of course, affected by many factors. By virtue of broad social forces a community may be going "up" or "down." The contribution of any social program to a community should be measured in terms of where the community is relative to where it would have been in the absence of the program. If statistical series are available for the community for a reasonable period of time (and one believes the data), an extrapolation can be made from the time the program began to estimate where it would have been in the absence of the program at the time of the evaluation. This has seldom been done.

Similarly, some might say we have chosen a type of program for which it is especially difficult to measure social benefits, but we would ask whether aid to a high school, renovation of an apartment building, or establishment of a day-care center would be any easier to evaluate. At any rate, we chose this deliberately to illustrate an instance in which one might want to settle for a process audit rather than insist on a performance measure.

Here we may pause for a moment to consider the implications of the use of the audit for internal and for external purposes. Internally, the firm may want an estimate, however crude, of the social contribution of its program and may rely on whatever data that are available and on informed judgment, possibly of an outside expert, on the various items we have enumerated or even some crude approximation thereof. If the firm is seriously assessing its programs, this judgment will assuredly be better than no information at all. However, if that judgment alone were used in public reporting, it might well be suspect as self-serving. Partial data, while of aid for internal decision making, might mislead, or be accused of misleading, the public.

Granted the above, the public might be served (and satisfied) as well as is feasible (or necessary, as it perceives the term) by a process audit that would include: a statement of the bank's perception of the nature and causes of the problems of minority businesses; a statement of the actions which might be taken to remedy those problems together with a spelling out of the rationale; a specification of the objectives of the program; enumeration of the resources committed to the program; detailing of the specific actions of the program together with an explication of how the bank's program fits into the broader remedial picture referred to above and a description of how they plan to evaluate it. The detailing of the actions of the program would include such matters as: loan policies in terms of interest charged and degree of acceptable risk; criteria for selecting businesses to invest in and degree of success in meeting those criteria; supporting activities such as technical assistance to or training programs for minority business owners, and the like. Partial performance measures such as numbers and volume of loans, ratio of successful to unsuccessful loans (if there is a reportable track record) and so on, would be reported, but not with the implication that such partial measures were a full basis for judging the "social contribution" of the program.

With an audit of this sort, an outsider could compare the bank's program with that of other banks in terms of level of effort and degree of sophistication and evidence of a continuing commitment. To the extent that the outsider had a competent knowledge of the problems of minority businesses, he could judge the probability of its success. A program that was at an appropriate level of effort and conformed to the best understanding of the problem would by definition be as good a program as could be mounted. Whether *any* program could attain the stated objectives, and therefore whether or not such a program should be undertaken at all, would be a matter of further judgment.

In principle, the process audit, like many other things, seems straightforward. It needs to be tried so that we may find out what its complications are. Questions that occur are: which programs ought to be audited primarily in terms of effects, and which primarily in process terms, and how may this vary by circumstances? Or can (and should) some projects be audited by both methods? How may knowledge of "best practice" be built into audit teams? To what extent is such knowledge necessary? This type of knowledge is presently the province of individual specialists. Furthermore, in many instances there is likely to be little agreement on best practice. Can the process description be sufficiently standardized across firms and across practices so that meaningful comparisons can be made? Or can the credibility of a group of individuals be so generally accepted that their "findings" will be taken as valid?

Incidentally, a meaningful question which falls out of the orientation toward "solving social problems" as opposed to either satisfying one's conscience or staying out of trouble is the extent to which the businessman takes the initiative in selecting his target as compared to following general practice or responding to the demands made on his particular firm. Certainly the popular conception is that in the past he has taken this initiative in the area of corporate giving. The legend has it that corporate giving is largely affected by the charitable preferences of the sitting president's wife. On a less frivolous level, it is quite obvious that some corporations have shown general preferences for some types of social programs where the choice has not been forced on them by the demands of the environment—though these preferences may often simply reflect the personal concerns of past chief executives now frozen into tradition. Considering the extent to which individual social programs of businesses have had varying success, there seems little doubt that improvement can be made in matching the firm's resources to the selection of social problems to be tackled, and in designing better ways of meeting the chosen objective. Such an analysis should follow from the findings of a social audit. However, this does suggest that one of the elements of the audit ought to be an assessment of the wisdom of the choices the firm has made in the objective it has pursued. This will involve delving into the question of just how the decision to embark on the program was made so that the rationale of that choice may be compared to the rationale of other choices. By and large, the evidence suggests that companies "fall into" these programs rather than select them rationally from the hundreds of alternatives presented to them.

Increased Long-Range Profits   The final potential objective we have attributed to the businessman's acceptance of social responsibility is that he wants to increase profits. Certainly the most prevailing stated justification for socially responsible actions is that they "contribute to long-run profitability." In most instances this is an exceedingly complicated calculation to make. In some instances it is not. If the socially responsible action has been legislated, and the penalties of violation (either direct or indirect) are higher than the benefits of evasion, and the chances of enforcement are sufficiently high, then the answer is clear. Or, certain actions may be necessary to ensure survival in a community, though operationally this may translate itself into a question of how much community pressure the manager himself can personally tolerate. If we assume that he or someone reasonably like him is essential for running the firm, then we may further assume that the response is necessary for the survival of the firm, and thereby contributed to its long-range profitability.

Let us assume, however, that the purpose of a social audit is to enable management to take steps that will increase the company's profitability either by raising or lowering their investment in socially responsible action and/or by choosing more "efficient" social programs. Again, simple straightforward situations might be found. One consulting firm found a company that was subsidizing an athletic team to the tune of tens of thousands of dollars annually without even the benefit of being identified with the team. About half that sum would have made a considerable contribution to cleaning up the town's water supply. However, such gross cases are obviously not particularly interesting. We will first look at what would be required to "optimize" profitability and then consider some more modest objectives.

An audit designed to meet the objective of optimizing profitability would have certain information needs that are easy to specify. They are: the true costs of present programs, the dollar contribution to profitability over some specified time period of each of these programs; the true costs of alternate programs that might be considered; and the dollar contribution of each of the alternate programs.[13] In then making the calculation of the optimum program package one would, of course, take into due consideration the increased uncertainty of the estimates of costs and contributions of as yet untried programs, together with the interactive effects of all plausible packages.

The logic of the above passage is impeccable. Its operational feasibility is at best dubious.

There are several ways in which a corporation's socially responsible activities may contribute to its profitability. It is said that social responsibility is a precondition for survival, if not of the individual business firm, of the business system as a whole. It is also argued that social responsibility makes it possible for a firm to attract a superior type of employee. Social responsibility makes a firm attractive to at least some investors. Social responsibility may attract some customers to a firm's products or services. Finally, socially responsible actions should contribute to making the local community and the society at large a better place in which to do business.

Informed judgments on all these potential contributions can be made. And such judgments may be extremely valuable for internal decision making. However, the question facing us at this point is the extent to which such contributions can be expressed in terms of dollar contribution to profits.

Certain of these contributions may in fact be converted into reasonable dollar estimates. For example, a survey of consumers might reveal what proportion were patronizing the firm's goods or services because of its image for social responsibility.[14] If, however, the firm's social programs added to the prices of its goods and services, an estimate would also have to be made of the proportion of potential customers who were lost because of this circumstance. The same might be done with investors. Such information, which could reasonably well be converted into estimates of dollar

---

[13] These parallel the requirement for "solving social problems" except here our performance measure is "dollar contribution to profitability" rather than "social contribution."

[14] If the experiences of black businesses which had counted on preferential treatment from inner-city customers is any guide, this number is likely to be painfully small!

contribution to profits, would be rather expensive to come by if precise sampling methods were used.

Except in extreme cases (e.g., a plant might be threatened with being shut down because of violating a local ordinance, or be closed down temporarily by picketing militants), it is difficult to comprehend the full dimensions of "survival." While the dollar consequences of failing to survive might be calculable if the time of future demise were known, the contribution of any one firm to the survival of the American business system (one of the benefits that presumably flows from social responsibility) would not.

With a good deal of work, it seems credible that one might be able to estimate the dollar benefits accruing from recruiting superior employees. This might be complicated by the circumstance that being "socially responsible" would include hiring employees for whom at least the initial training period would be more expensive than for other employees who might be hired—a figure that would have to be balanced off against the higher profit performance the company could expect from the improved caliber of its executive recruits. But even without this complication, it strikes us that measuring the increased corporate benefits achieved by hiring Mr. P. B. Kappa as opposed to Mr. Gentleman's See could be a pretty messy accounting problem.

Finally, we consider the dollar value of contributing to a more viable community or society. We have previously seen how difficult it can be to measure the *social* contribution of at least some of a firm's social programs. To convert such social contributions into dollar contributions to the firm would be doubly difficult. There can be no doubt that a firm profits by doing business in a prosperous and healthy community and society. But, to trace the effects of its own actions through the chain of social causality, except in the simplest of situations, seems about as impossible as anything we can imagine.

The full task of conducting a social audit for "optimizing" a corporation's profit[15] would be formidable and is not likely to be undertaken in the near future by a well advised firm.

---

[15] Such an audit would obviously be made in the first instance for internal decision making. It is interesting to speculate on what the reaction would be if the results were made public. Certainly there would be some attraction in revealing them to stockholders and potential investors or lenders. Such an effort would communicate the image of an enlightened and probably profitable company. It is by no means certain that the general public would react favorably. If the audit worked as it was intended, it would reveal such things as a decision to shift funds from program A to program B because the latter contributed more to the firm's long-range profits. Is this "social responsibility"?

But, once more we have taken the task very literally and outlined the logical implications of what would be meant by conducting an audit to optimize a firm's long-range profits. The use of the heroic term "optimize" ought always to be suspect in such contexts. Few executives have the illusion that even their regular business decisions are "optimal." If we set ourselves the more modest goal of "improving" profitability, the task becomes somewhat more feasible. But, since a firm might well choose to forego foreseeable profits in the interests of some socially responsible policy, we propose that the goal of making financially better advised decisions be employed. This goal is certainly attainable, and attainable at varying levels of modesty or ambition.

Most firms probably cannot display even the out-of-pocket costs of all of their activities that could fall under the rubric of social responsiveness for the appropriate executives to contemplate. Few firms know the true costs of their programs even approximately. Probably many firms would benefit from a review of the decisions to enter the programs they presently have ("how did we even get into this?").

While we have taken a discouraging view of getting a definitive measure of the social contribution of some (or most) types of socially responsible programs, we have also pointed to the possibility of partial measures and/or informed judgments. We have little doubt that almost any firm would benefit from having available for its officers' contemplation a more systematic display of partial measures and informed judgments on the worth of its programs both from the point of view of the society and the interests of the firm. How far it should go with this is, in turn, a matter of judgment as to what costs and efforts are justified at a particular time.

Added to the above, any knowledge of the expectations of various publics and of their perceptions of what the firm is doing, would aid executive decisions.

Auditing for Internal Decisions—Summarized   The various types of audits that might be conducted to serve various corporate motives are in a sense cumulative. One could stop at various points along the line. The audit to satisfy the executive's conscience is the least demanding. By definition it is complete when his conscience is satisfied. Whether the audit to anticipate and avoid pressure or that for measuring one's social contribution should be next in line is moot. But, it is clear that making financially better advised decisions would benefit from the information of all of the preceding types of audits. One might argue that a diligent attempt to improve one's social contribution would include making financially wise decisions. However, logically they are separable, particularly if one includes the possibility that an executive might, if making a financially better informed decision, decide to lower his social contribution. We treated them separately for this reason, and also because we wanted to explore the more ambitious possibility of auditing to optimize long-range profits.

With the exception of the audit to satisfy the corporate conscience, we found the logical extension of any of these audits (or audit modules) to be demanding and expensive if indeed they are possible at all—so much so that the logical extension would seldom be pursued. But in each instance we also found that there are many fall-back positions of varying degrees of adequacy. Considering that it is generally conceded that business decisions apropos regular business matters could be almost universally improved, it seems highly likely that any increased systematization of the newer, more muddled area of decisions concerning socially responsive actions would be beneficial.

Since the auditing we have been discussing is intended for internal decision making, the degree of adequacy, the costs one is willing to incur, and the extent to which one is content to rely on various forms of judgment are appropriately up to the discretion of the executives of the corporation.

There is, of course, no one answer as to what is the appropriate level of effort except in the context of the situation of a particular firm in a particular industry with a particular set of programs and executives at a given level of development of the art of social auditing. It can only be anticipated that individual firms that attempt social auditing for internal decision making will go through a period of trial and error in which they find certain procedures useful, and certain levels of effort appropriate. The fact that one must now, and perhaps forever, rely on approximations of the measures we would like ideally, or on process descriptions in the absence of output measures, need be cause for no concern at this stage. If social auditing does in fact grow, we may expect it to parallel the history of regular financial accounting in which imprecise measures were sorted out, and the surviving measures retained because of their utility which, in turn, was enhanced through usage.

For various reasons not everything that might be used in auditing for internal decision making would be appropriate for public reporting. Whether the true costs of social programs should or will be reported to stockholders is a matter that may evolve out of

66

negotiations (probably implicit) between the parties or out of corporate officers' sense of their responsibilities to the stockholders. Many of the judgments that officers may be willing to rely on for their own decisions would not be accepted as adequate by the public—though we suspect this is less true of the process audit. Finally, as we have hinted (in footnote 14), information used and decisions made to increase the financial wisdom of corporate social policies might be of interest to stockholders, but might backfire with the general public if, as is likely, the corporation's social concerns were revealed as tempered at least in part by financial considerations.

AUDITING FOR PUBLIC REPORTING. The most challenging of the visions of the corporate social audit sees the day when business firms will regularly report their performance in areas of social responsibility as regularly as they do financial performance. This vision is illustrated by the following passage from *The Wall Street Journal* of December 9, 1971:

> D. S. Langsdorf, senior vice president and comptroller of the Bank of America, predicts that within three to five years annual reports will be required to include data on a company's social outlays. Some authorities foresee complete "social audits" of firms by outside consultants within a decade, just as outside accountants conduct financial audits today. *Business and Society,* a biweekly newsletter that reports on corporate social involvement, predicts that eventually ratings of a company's "social performance" will be as readily available as ratings of its credit-worthiness.

The *Journal* itself hints at an even more ambitious objective when it asks:

> How, for instance, can a profit-and-loss statement be made to reflect the good a company does by assigning some of its personnel to advising minority businessmen struggling to succeed in a ghetto? How can the installation of pollution-control devices at a factory be shown at the bottom line as a positive accomplishment rather than a drain on productivity?

The notion that somehow social performance will be integrated with financial performance envisions that a baby which has not yet started to crawl will some day run. We will look at the prospects of its walking. We may at this point note that the baby has at least begun to crawl inasmuch as quite a few corporations are presently discussing their social programs in their annual reports, in their advertising, and in special publications. Such reporting, however, is by no means universal, nor is it comprehensive (in that it covers the full range of issues in which the public is interested), nor is it always credible, nor is it always interpretable even though it may be believed.

We shall be able to say that public corporate social audits are a *fait accompli* when such auditing is widespread, periodic, reasonably comprehensive (you can't please everybody), credible, and its meaning is reasonably clear. This will depend on the degree to which corporations are motivated to make their social record public, how the data gathering and reporting are done, on the answers to certain technical questions, and on the cost and effort of making audits that will satisfy the requirements of the public. It also depends on the coalescence of public attitudes around some generally accepted yardsticks.

A corporation may well be in a quandary as to whether or not it wants to make its social record public. Most of those presently attempting audits clearly want to evaluate the picture that emerges before they decide to publicize it. However, this question may be the one which is most easily resolved.

Corporations have not been particularly successful in hiding from the public any key aspects of their social performance (costs are another matter). Much is open to direct public scrutiny: composition of a sales force, pollution of air and water, military contracts, sales or investments in South Africa, and so on. Beyond this, public interest champions have succeeded in opening up a considerable portion of material that the firms they have attacked wish was not public. The Council on Economic Priorities seems to find out most of what it seeks to find or successfully embarrasses the firms that will not cooperate. And, in general, there is now a fair-sized group of newsletters that publish information on corporate social responsibility or irresponsibility as the editors define it.

Additionally, reporting requirements imposed by the government might increase. As we have indicated, the SEC, in its ruling of July 1971, compels firms offering new stock issues to reveal if they are under indictment for pollution or for employment discrimination, or if they have pollution problems that would involve considerable capital expense to correct. The Equal Employment Opportunity Commission gets regular reports on the employment status of women and minorities from government contractors and might be persuaded to make these reports public. Finally, some perceptible, though not precisely definable, portion of the investment community is interested in the social performance of the firms in which

it invests. (One cannot help but assume that those responsible for many institutional portfolios, like universities and churches, temper their choices by such concerns whether or not they explicitly admit it.)

The idea that firms would or could resist disclosure for long is not self-evident. Obviously the reluctance still exists and may persist for some time. However, unless public concern diminishes or the public interest "auditors" (including the less systematic one-shot gadflys) somehow fall out of public favor or lose their zeal, the motivation for and possibility of concealment will atrophy.

On the issue of how data should be gathered and reported, it seems a reasonable guess that over the long run—if the corporate social audit is taken seriously—there will be pressure for this task to be undertaken or certified by outside auditors. (This may mean auditors in the current sense of the term, or perhaps a group of professionals in social programs. One can speculate, for example, that the process audit might become the province of a new profession.) Already, too many people are circulating the story of the anti-pollution ad that featured the picture of a river taken upstream from the polluting plant, or of the automobile company that proclaimed that it was "voluntarily" complying with the California state law. Nevertheless, one must not rule out the possibility that audits self-done and self-reported will gain credibility. This depends on how they are done and on what issues.

We cannot foresee how this balance will work out and, to a large degree, it depends on the performance of business itself. Most probably the first public audits will be made without such outside certification. We must observe the response.

There are those who are skeptical that even independently certified public audits will be credible. They take this position on the grounds that the information contained in them would be designed more to influence the public than to reveal any true state of affairs. One must assume that companies would not needlessly cast themselves in a bad light, and we may look at the parallel in financial reporting, which is already known for its flexibility for representing a firm's financial status in a positive fashion. But the accounting profession is constantly striving, under the stimulus of public pressure, to tighten up its standards for financial reporting, and the important point is that the existing system which has evolved over a long period of time, continues to be generally accepted despite its imperfections. It is not too much to expect the same, ultimately, of the social audit.

If public corporate social auditing is to become a regular process, we would of course expect the development of standards to be evolutionary, and we would expect that evolution to take many years. It will probably be argued that data pertaining to social performance are less "hard" and therefore easier to fudge than are financial data. But, it could be equally plausible to argue in return that the evidence for social performance is more accessible to those who dig for it than is financial data. And, of course, we have plenty of evidence that there are those who are digging for it. As a result, the presence of public interest auditors would be a source of pressure for honesty in reporting, and a source of correction where reporting was not honest. Considering these offsetting circumstances, it is not possible to say whether social auditing—in whatever shape it finally emerges—would shape up more or less rapidly than financial auditing.

All this assumes, of course, that we can conquer the kinds of problems cited in this chapter. The technical aspects of a publicly reported social audit involve most of the complexities of one made for internal decision making. It is, after all, the identical thicket. But there is an additional consideration here which puts a strain on many of the compromises a firm might make for internal use, a strain we have hinted at in an earlier discussion of the internal decision-making audit. We refer to the tricky question of what the public wants reported and how much detail they require.

Take the question of the financial wisdom of specific social programs, for example. As we have suggested, the general public would be least likely to demand or be interested in close calculations on this subject. The investing public, one could assume, will react positively to the inclusions of at least some data. The evidence from the Boston study we have cited would indicate that the general public, while not caring about detail, would react positively to evidence that the company had made such calculations. It would strike them as being a serious, businesslike approach and, since they assume (with approval, not cynicism) that a company will ultimately act in its own self-interest, they would likely see in a positive determination of the corporate benefits of Program A as opposed to Program B a guarantee that the company will maintain it and handle it seriously instead of casually.

The point is, though, that both the investing community and the general public are likely to be satisfied with fairly minimal accounting along these lines. This means, in our view, that because this type of auditing is most demanding, the task of the ultimate social

70

audit suggested by *The Wall Street Journal*—an integration of social and financial performance—is not likely to be addressed for some time.

By the same token, if a firm does the sort of political and social analysis we suggested as a possibility for anticipating and avoiding pressure, it will presumably not wish to show it. But here again, it is conveivable that the public will want evidence that it has systematically reviewed its constituent's concerns, both internal and external, and adjusted its course accordingly. If that proves to be the case, the corporation will be forced to—and maybe even find it advantageous to—make its findings available.

There is another possibility: that the public will demand more data than a company needs for its own purposes. In our previous discussion we raised many technical problems, inherent in determining the true cost of existing programs, let alone in measuring and evaluating their effects. Time after time, we pointed to fallback positions, most often turning on the substitution of informed judgment when data were not available, or the use of partial data supported by judgment when complete data could not be developed. Many of the compromises which one might willingly make for his own decision making could fall short of what is required for credible public reporting. One must guess that the public will stress "objectivity" and "completeness" in what is reported to them.

At first glance, the probable public demand for more objective and full reporting might seem to place an insuperable demand on social auditing. We believe, however, that the public is likely to be quite satisfied with measures of social performance which fall far short of many of the idealized audits we have previously discussed. For example, while the corporation may indeed want to know what the true costs of corporate giving programs are, the public may well only be interested in the out-of-pocket costs, since this is the measure of what is "given." The public is likely to want to know the causes to which the corporation has given money, and those in which it has involved itself, and to be content with evidence that the corporation is making some kind of continuing effort to assess whether or not these "causes" are effective in serving their avowed purpose. It may well not require the evaluations themselves. After all, the public will in all probability have made its own judgment on this matter, a judgment that may or may not correspond to what a more sophisticated assessment would invoke. Moreover, in many areas, the public will be content with a statement of what is being *done,* as contrasted to what is being accomplished (e.g., mortgage loans in the ghetto).[16] Here is where process audits would come in. Finally, in some areas it is easy to produce objective and apparently complete measures of performance (if not useable comparative data)—such as minority and female employment practices, and pollution abatement. And, measures of performance are likely to be demanded in such areas.

We would point out that we have here made fairly educated guesses as to what standards of reporting the public will respond to favorably in various social areas. But they are, at best, guesses. This is a question susceptible to research, and such research should be done.

But the issue goes beyond the *kind* of reporting the public will find acceptable and informative. One cannot except the matter of the *context* in which the public will evaluate what is reported. Particularly pertinent are the norms against which a firm's performance is judged, a matter to which we have already alluded. We have cited Sater's suggestion of four types of norms that he would include in an audit: performance by other companies in the industry, by similar firms in the same geographic location, local legal requirements, and some norm of what is possible in a given location (e.g., minority employment as a function of the proportion and education of minority group members in the area). One can well imagine that the inclusion of such a set of norms would enhance the interpretibility of a firm's reported performance. However, as we have indicated, such norms are sparsely and unevenly available. Probably if social auditing matures, it will be accompanied by a gradual accretion of more adequate norms. Local (and state, and national) legal requirements are of course available, and the task is one of assembling and presenting them. Some norms on corporate giving are available and could be improved. For example, norms on minority and female employment are available in aggregate forms for firms that file EEO-1 forms, but they might be better assembled in different categories for the sorts of judgments that would be made of a social audit. Pollution laws vary and are unevenly enforced. Anti-pollution performance for industries is weakly developed, but may become more adequate as a result of investor and public interest audits. Other types of norms, such as for mortgage policies of banks and insurance companies do not, insofar as we know, exist in any form, nor do they

[16] There is evidence to show that the public has confidence in a company's ability to select worthwhile activities and carry them out. What they want is proof that businessmen are concerned and committed enough that they are doing the selecting and implementing with skill and care.

exist for aid to education or "corporate responsiveness" or "quality of life in the workplace." As with many other aspects of social auditing, we would expect the development of norms and the eventual selection of those which are most useful for audit evaluations to develop over time via various routes.

There will also be *ad hoc* circumstances that would or should affect the public judgment of a firm's social performance. For example, two paper mills, one with a fifty-year-old plant, and one with a brand new plant, would be judged differently if they had similar pollution records. We assume that such *ad hoc* circumstances cannot become part of a regular reporting ritual, but rather will be introduced as descriptive modifiers by each firm in commenting on its own performance.

Finally, of all the broad "technical" problems associated with public reporting, we turn last to that of coverage. What areas of social responsibility should a social audit include? As the reader no doubt expects, we take refuge in two of our favorite forms of evasion: the lack of any single clear answer, and the necessity to rely on evolution.

From the earlier sections of this report and from his own experience the reader knows that the list of candidates is very long, and the consensus as to what is essential is unfirm. At the end of 1971, minority and female employment practices, protection of the environment and, less often, corporate giving were on almost everyone's list. After that, the consensus weakens. We present the following list from an internal corporate memorandum as illustrative of how far the list might be extended:

1. Charitable giving—art, education, poverty, health, and anti-discrimination.
2. Employee benefits.
3. Community improvement.
4. Efforts to influence legislation, which might include political activity.
5. Minority hiring.
6. Protection of environment.
7. Method and type of advertising.
8. Standards for providing good and safe products for customers.
9. Method of selection of business the corporation conducts, for example, napalm and business in South Africa.
10. Health and safety of employees.
11. Make-up and duties of board of directors.
12. Matters relating to shareholder democracy such as methods of soliciting proxies and methods of nominating directors (including among methods of soliciting proxies) might be the extent to which

a corporation provides machinery for pass-through voting by fiduciaries and nominees.
13. The extent of reporting on matters that are not financially material within SEC standards but are of social significance.

It is amusing that despite the apparent diligence with which this list was compiled, the writer does not mention female employment! If it were worth the effort we could go back to some of the criteria suggested by the Public Affairs Council and the Dreyfus Third Century Fund and expand the list considerably. But there would be no point.

At this juncture, any company attempting a social audit will have to make a judgment of what it considers relevant to its peculiar circumstances, taking into consideration what it thinks the public to whom it is reporting thinks is relevant, and make a choice from the almost endless list of items that have been labeled "socially relevant." Hopefully, over time some consensus will emerge as to what a company in a given industry should report.

However, evolution will not be only toward consensus as to what should be reported. We must expect that there will also be an evolution of expectations. If one takes the recent past as a basis for predicting, he would have to guess that expectations will expand, that new standards of performance will be raised, and that new issues will be introduced. The content of audits may change over time not only because new issues arise, but because old issues become less relevant. Thus in the 1970's good labor relations are no longer much of an issue. Similarly, if pollution laws are made strict and are enforced, pollution control will not be a meaningful measure of corporate social performance unless either violations of the law or performance appreciably above legal requirements are sufficiently frequent to be of diagnostic value. Social responsibility is a moving target.

One issue that has concerned some writers on the subject of corporate social audits we would dismiss summarily. This is the notion of weighting areas of social performance to produce a composite index of social responsibility. The reason is simple but powerful. Such weights are matters of value judgments to be made by individuals. And individual preference schemes vary so widely that any one weighting scheme would deprive the users of audits of the opportunity to do what is proper—use their own weights. For one reader, involvement in South Africa is so heinous that it outweighs all that Company X is doing in its community. For another, minority employment programs are so generally accepted that Company Y gets no gold stars for that; the issue is internal democracy. We regard, then, the attempt to reach a determination as to whether this corporation or that is socially responsible as a waste of time and a misuse of the social audit concept.

Audits for Public Reporting—Summarized   If one were to pose the question simply, "what are the cost/benefits of a corporation making its social performance a matter of public knowledge?" the answer would probably be that the benefits would outweigh the costs providing the costs did not involve the price of preparing the report. The reasoning is simple. As it becomes increasingly difficult for the corporation to keep its social performance from the public, it becomes increasingly advantageous to be the agency for making the performance public both to demonstrate the corporation's good intent, and to insure that the record is presented in the most defensible terms. However, the only cost is not the social cost of having one's record known.

No one can answer what it costs to prepare a social audit because, as we have demonstrated, a social audit may mean many things. *The Wall Street Journal* article of December 7, 1971, quotes a bank executive as estimating the costs as ". . . about $75,000 in consultant fees plus 'an awful lot' of in-house time. You could go through a lot of expensive wheel-spinning and end up with nothing of value, he says." This may be regarded as illustrative of the money costs. If the reader wants to make a stab at what "an awful lot of in-house time" involves, he may imagine five to ten executives meeting at fairly regular intervals, clerks scurrying around gathering records, and quite possibly a revamping of the accounting system so that true costs can be determined. As we have often indicated, a more modest effort is possible, but this is what may be involved.

However, there is still another type of cost that we have not discussed in this chapter, but which we mentioned earlier: the internal consequences to the firm of doing the audit at all. Because the very act means invading the domain of corporate officers, and because the findings constitute a judgment on the performance of corporate officers, especially along a dimension on which they have not been measured heretofore, the conduct of an audit can and has generated internal friction. More fundamentally, attempts to conduct a social audit may surface deep philosophical differences among corporate officers. Our guess is that this internal cost may in some instances be considerable enough to slow up or stop the auditing process, or the prospect of it may be sufficient to discourage a firm from undertaking the effort.

The issue of internal organizational cost is likely to loom highest early in the history of corporate social audits for two reasons. The first is that early auditing attempts are likely to be clumsy and therefore consume more corporate energy and cause more corporate dislocation than might be true after the art of auditing is better developed, and all this in a climate where many executives will grump: "What's all this got to do with our business, anyway?" This is especially true in today's climate where the public demand for and interest in such an audit, though increasing, is a long way from being demonstrably irresistible. Thus the effort in a company, as we have said, still tends to be pretty much the plaything of the top man.

The second reason is that *if* social auditing becomes relatively well established, the rationale for a particular firm doing it will be easier to communicate, and therefore there will be a greater disposition to be willing to pay the organizational costs. We would, in any event, expect the early history of corporate social audits to proceed in fits and starts. Internal corporate friction will contribute to this.

While we have dwelled at length on the technical difficulties of developing social audits, we assume that they can be resolved if not solved—though we do not know when, how, or at what cost. Our reasoning is again simple. An ideal solution of all the technical problems, particularly at an early stage, is a manifest impossibility. What has to be striven for is that which is feasible and useful. Thus, the early difficulty will not be in the need for quickly solving all of the technical problems, but in reaching an agreement between auditor and user as to what is feasible and useful. This is a matter of social communication and the establishment of social trust. Considering the state of trust between the business community and the general public, this may be where the problem lies.

The Future of Investor and Public Interest Audits

The role of investor and public interest audits may eventually be regarded as ancillary to that of corporate self-audits. They provide evidence that is not readily available from the corporations themselves, and if the information becomes increasingly available from the corporations the role of investor and public interest audits will wane or change. At the present time, one of the most important consequences of investor and public interest audits is to serve as a stimulus for the development of corporate self-audits. In this context, it must be added that public interest gadflys, while not concerned with broad continuing evaluation of firms' social performance, have an equal stimulus value.

However, investor and public interest audits have the more immediate tasks of providing investors with knowledge of the social responsibility of firms in which they might invest, and providing the general public with information on the social performance both of specific firms and of business in general (though the latter chiefly by implication). To the extent that the general and investing publics continue to be interested in the issue of businesses' social responsibilities the requirement for such information will continue.

One must assume, even if the practice of corporate self-auditing grows, that it will be a long time before it becomes sufficiently regular, systematic, and widespread to serve the needs of the general and investing publics. Hence we must anticipate that investor and public interest auditing will be with us for some time over the foreseeable future, unless there is a surprising drop in interest in corporate social responsibility.

The ranks of investor auditors may be swelled. If the present socially responsible mutual funds prosper, others may join their ranks. At present, a number of major foundations, churches, and universities are examining the social aspects of their investment policies. They may set up their own auditing facility. Individual officers of a number of large brokerage firms are doing some form of social auditing. Trust officers of banks are being asked to assemble "clean" portfolios. The market for investor auditing will grow in proportion to the number of large investors who are interested in socially responsible investment. There is a probability of pooled auditing in the case of nonprofit institutions such as foundations and churches which are not in competition with each other. We assume that mutual funds and brokerage houses will do their own auditing for competitive reasons.

While we may guess that investor audits may increase over the near future, we can be less confident of what will happen with public interest audits. To the extent that a public interest auditor is tied to a particular constituency, such as the National Council of Churches, it will probably be assured of continuing financial support. However, th future of an organization such as the Council on Economic Priorities, dependent on pluralistic support from subscribers and sponsors, is less certain. If one uses as a model the success of Ralph Nader in financing an ever-widening collection of activities, he would be sanguine. But, any such organization is dependent on the zeal of dedicated people and their willingness to continue to work long hours for little money. This may not be the deciding factor in the end; after all, our society is populated by all kinds of special-interest groups that struggle and survive. The crucial question is public interest, confidence, and acceptance. Without that, the groups may continue but their leverage will be gone.

Over the near future the contribution of the public interest groups will probably be to develop new issues and test the degree of public interest in those issues, which the more systematic auditors may or may not add to their portfolio of concerns.

We can see no force at work which would push investor and public interest auditors to uniformity of coverage or methods, or toward any other form of comparability of standardization, in the immediate future. Hence, we may expect continued heterogeneity dependent on the interests and resources of the auditor.

The investor and public interest auditors, by and large, share the technical problems of corporate self-auditors in all save that of credibility in public reporting. However, the public interest and investor auditors may not share some of the concerns which corporations might have for internal decision making. As we have indicated, public interest auditors may have no desire to know true costs of social programs except to the extent that this measure might develop as an index of corporate commitment. Investor auditors, while having a potential interest in true costs, and the cost/effectiveness of social programs, are likely to be content with the record of overall financial performance without knowing to what extent this is dependent on cost/effective social policies.

However, the investor and particularly the public interest auditors have additional technical problems stemming from that of access to information internal to the corporation. (Not that the internal audits are totally free of that problem, as we have noted!) The access of investor auditors will vary according to the amount of leverage the auditor has on the firms it wishes to audit. For example, a socially responsible fund that is affiliated with well established regular funds is likely to have better access than a new unaffiliated fund concerned with socially responsible investment. However, the example of the public interest auditors and of the public interest groups indicates that ingenuity and diligence can do a great deal to conquer the problem of access. Furthermore, it is difficult to see any trends in the future that will increase the difficulty of this problem. If anything the government may extend reporting responsibilities of corporations, and corporations may find it less and less viable to refuse to respond to inquiries.

In sum, our best guess is that the investor and public interest auditors will be with us in the future barring that eventual millennium in which regular corporate auditing will displace their function, or an unanticipated change in the atmosphere, making them either unacceptable or uninteresting to the public. Their continued activity will continue to make that day more likely, but scarcely inevitable.

Needs for Research and Development

We have repeatedly recorded our uncertainty as to the future of
the concept of the corporate social audit. However, if it develops
along any one or combination of the lines implied in the preceding
chapters, the course of that development may be facilitated by the
acquisition of certain understanding, knowledge, and skill which
we will try to identify in this chapter. For practical purposes, all
new social innovations have grown to date on an *ad hoc* basis
without the aid of such social research and development. It is our
faith that the deliberate development of such knowledge and skills
could enable an innovation like this one to evolve in a more orderly
fashion.

The concept of and interest in the social audit is a concrete
indicator of a much larger phenomenon: the changing role of the
corporation, with specific reference to the increased demands that
it be more socially responsive. If it were not for this change, there
would be no call for a social audit. The program of research and
development that we propose is cast in this broader context, since
it is only in this context that we can understand what is expected
of the corporation, what the consequences of those expectations
may be, how the corporation responds to social demands, and
thereby the purposes that an audit may serve, and the changes that

may take place in corporate and public responses as a result of auditing.

Our proposed program of research and development will begin with matters central to the corporate social audit itself and proceed in later sections of the chapter to issues of the broader context of the audit.

I. *Developmental History of Social Auditing*

The idea of a corporate social audit may be akin to a number of other recent business fashions such as operations research, management information systems, management by objectives, sensitivity training, PERT, and the like. Such innovations have a characteristic history both across and within firms. These developments pass through stages of: getting acquainted, trial and enthusiasm; disillusionment over the difficulties and failure to produce utopian results; and then consolidation and equilibrium. The accompanying literature goes through similar waves. The early literature suffers from what has been labeled "tense error." Enthusiastic programmatic notions are presented as though they were descriptions of presently ongoing systems. This is followed by a wave of debunking literature, and then by a wave in which the innovation is treated realistically. The early history of such innovations is marked by acute organizational and technical problems, as well as by unrealistic expectation.

RESEARCH TOPICS. The developmental history of the corporate social audit ought to be tracked closely, partially as a matter of social history, but equally importantly for the identification and diagnosis of the organizational and technical problems that arise. In general, when such innovations have been attempted, organizational problems have been given a back-of-the-hand treatment, largely because they have been promoted and developed by persons competent and interested in their technical features who are not particularly competent, interested in, appreciative of, or comfortable with organizational matters. There is, therefore, reason to pay careful attention to the organizational dimensions of the social audit.

The early history of this innovation could be tracked by following the literature, establishing broad contacts with persons involved in the movement, and by as detailed a case study of particular audits as is feasible. Feasibility will be conditioned by problems of access. Most of the firms presently trying audits exhibit a considerable amount of shyness.

Perhaps the auditors within the firm can be persuaded to keep a diary. Or, they can be debriefed at regular intervals. Each of these procedures has its drawbacks. Keeping a diary may be an impossible addition to a busy person's workload. Debriefing involves the bias of selective recall, but nevertheless does offer some opportunity to learn. Eventually one would hope to have an observer who could monitor several audits on a relatively continuing basis, sitting in on meetings, observing procedures, and the like.

Many firms which are not conducting an audit on a formal, across the board sense, are executing components of an audit: monitoring the firm's advertising; reviewing corporate giving; evaluating manpower programs; and the like. These programs, as well as the public interest and investor audits, should be studied for what they can teach us about auditing. Priority should be given to those components for which there is at least accumulated experience. It may also be anticipated that even the execution of individual components of an audit will reveal organizational problems.

From this monitoring would come a picture of the corporate social audit as a social as well as a technical process. It would also be a very good means of continually reassessing the research and development needs of the concept, as well as of ideas for better implementing it.

II. The Auditing Process

A series of activities can be foreseen which would facilitate the development of social auditing *per se*. They would scarcely be called "research" in the ordinary sense. Here, too, the word "development" is more appropriate.

RESEARCH TOPICS.   1. As we have noted a number of times, ascertainment of the true costs of social programs is an important component of a social audit both for understanding the wisdom of various resource allocations, and as a measure of the firm's level of effort in a given area. Whereas direct costs are readily identifiable, the allocation of indirect costs associated with a social program is ordinarily much more difficult because most accounting systems are designed not to permit their isolation. Furthermore, more than one convention for allocating indirect costs is likely to be plausible. Even in the area of regular financial accounting there is more than one reasonable way of allocating overhead. Appropriate methodologies for identifying indirect costs should be developed, and alternate conventions of allocation explored. These explorations should be made in terms of the various uses to which they would be put. For example, one procedure might be more useful for making internal cost/benefit decisions, while another might be judged as presenting to the public a "truer" indication of the level of effort. One method might be appropriate to some industries, but not to others.

Additionally, concepts should be developed for assessing the costs of alternate programs and the opportunity costs of alternate uses of the money, and methods appropriate to these concepts should be devised. Attempts at ascertaining "true" and "alternate" cost should proceed in two steps. The first should consist of understanding the problems and alternate procedures as well as possible. The second would be to develop practical procedures which were transferable and repeatable by others in different settings.

2. Relatively little attention has been paid to the task of auditing a firm's conduct of its regular business in a systematic way for its social consequences, though much of the criticism of business has been on this score, and the critics of business have been very capable in "auditing" business on this score in an *ad hoc* manner. We refer here to product safety, performance, durability, and to marketing and advertising practices, to the social desirability of products themselves (cigarettes, feminine hygiene deodorants) and so on. There are no proposals as to how one would go about such an audit in a systematic fashion or what norms should be used (other than compliance with the law). A checklist which might be followed is: the social utility of the firm's product line (a conceptually very difficult issue); quality of performance on their primary functions; secondary adverse (e.g., safety) or beneficial (e.g., aesthetic) effects; reasonableness of costs; advertising and marketing practice.

Exercises could be undertaken in auditing firms from a range of industries presenting a variety of different issues. For example, lending policies would be relevant for banks; product safety for toy manufacturers, reliability and safety for appliance manufacturers; exploration and exploitation practices for oil companies; and the like. Again, the aim would be to develop procedures that could be used by others.

3. In the body of this report we built the case for process auditing in instances where performance measures are extremely hard or expensive or where the effects of an action may be deferred beyond the point at which an evaluation has to be made. We need to develop experience in process auditing to decide for which types of

programs process audits are most appropriate, what types of evidence are available and appropriate, how it might be presented, what is credible and useful for the audience for which it is intended —whether it be for internal decision making, or for public reporting. Such a process audit would ascertain the following: the reason for undertaking a particular program, the goals of the program, the rationale for the action, a description of what is actually being done, and intermediate measures of performance if they are available.

4. While we have been skeptical of some more elaborate proposals for assessing the overall dollar contribution to the firm of all its socially responsible behavior, we concluded that more modest objectives are possible and may be desirable. Attempts should be made to do this. We suggest three reasonable candidates: improved recruiting as a result of the firm's socially responsible image; improved consumer acceptability; improved investor acceptability. It is quite widely asserted (and apparently believed, if we take the wave of advertisements claiming social responsibility as evidence) that these benefits accrue. One of the reasons for which social audits are advocated is that the most responsible firms will receive the benefits from their behavior. If this is true, it should be ascertained, if it is possible to do so.

5. Specific dollar contribution to a firm's profits as a result of its social programs will be impossible to determine in most instances. However, some programs, or some ways of executing the same programs, may be more efficient than others. By efficiency is meant the relationship between the cost of a program, in dollars or executive time and energy (which may be a scarer resource than money) and the amount of "good"—however measured—that is done. Even though such assessments may in part be judgmental, they ought to prove valuable to a firm in deciding where to put its efforts. Such exercises should be undertaken.

6. The range of issues involved in present conceptions of corporate social responsibility is highly diverse. Even if we bypass the more politico/philosophical issues such as investment in South Africa, producing munitions, lending money to Portugal, and so on, we are confronted by air, water, and noise pollution; black capitalism, hiring and training of minorities, employment and pay status of women; community development; physical rehabilitation of cities; support of various levels of education, day-care centers, drug abuse; crime; mass transportation; the impact of plant location on population distribution; consumerism; advertising and

marketing practices; contributions to various forms of charity; employee safety; employee benefits; product safety; and so on.

Each of these topics has its own area of expertise, its own norms of performance, and the like. No one person is in a position to give good advice as to what sort of program is most advisable for a given company in more than a few of these areas, nor is any one person entirely competent to judge a company's performance in more than a few of these areas. Ideally, one might envisage a "Handbook of Social Responsibility" that would offer uniform guidance to corporate officers to make wise decisions, to auditors to make appropriate audits, and for investors and the general public to make informed evaluations. This is probably an impossible task, and might be very inefficient to undertake at this point. However, a modest version—the beginnings of a series of short volumes—may be practical and useful.[17] For example, there is a body of experience of what works and what does not in business aid to public education, in day-care centers, in housing ventures, in aid of all sorts to minority business, in affirmative action and training programs. By the same token, there are people with expertise on consumer activities, on corporate organization for social programs, on project selection. This material could be pulled together in operationally useable form.

7. As the history of social audits unfolds, it is reasonable to expect that some issues will prove to be both relatively salient and relatively difficult. If there is the continued monitoring of the development of social audits, it is likely that from time to time social auditing will be in need of specific "technical assistance." Some agency should be prepared to respond to this need, whether it be in the form of convening a conference of people who need help and can offer help, the preparation of a monograph, the compilation of a list of resources to whom one can turn, or whatever seems in order. This may be an appropriate role of the Russell Sage Foundation itself.

8. We have stressed *ad nauseam* the variety of directions which the social audit might take. Furthermore, we have intuitive reservations concerning the probable consequences of firms contemplating any ambitious version of an audit at this time. These reservations are dual. The prospect of an ambitious audit is likely to appear so

[17] An example of what such volumes might look like is Jules Cohn's *The Conscience of the Corporations: Business and Urban Affairs, 1967–1970*, The Johns Hopkins Press, Baltimore, 1971. In our judgment this book is not as penetrating as it might be. It does, however, attempt to pull together business experience in one area of social responsibility.

formidable or threatening that the probability of attempting an audit will be low. And, an ambitious audit attempt stands a high risk of failure for both technical and organizational reasons, thereby producing no positive results and reducing the possibility of anything being done at a later date.

There is, however, a very modest version of an audit that is reasonably demanding but which should prove valuable at a low risk to the firm. It would consist of four steps: development of an inventory of the firm's activities that have a social impact; exploration of the circumstances ("reasons" may be too dignified a term) that generated these activities; an informal evaluation of those activities for which expert opinion is relevant (e.g., a minority hiring program); judgmental assessment of the fit of these activities with the objectives of the firm and the society.

Carrying a few firms through this exercise might be a good vehicle for doing some of the research we have advocated (e.g., on understanding the rationale of existing programs) while giving the firms a motive for cooperating. It would also provide better understanding of the problems of making an inventory of social programs (such as deciding what to include, how to gather data on executive community activities, and the like), relating social programs to business plans, and so on.

III. Reporting of Audits

In general, we do not know what form of public reporting is credible to the relevant publics for audits, how they will interpret the data, what norms they will consider relevant, and so on.

RESEARCH TOPICS. 1. Experiments can be conducted with alternate forms of reporting (performance, process, level of effort) for various social programs. As we have pointed out previously, technical feasibility may favor one type of audit over the others. Hopefully there would be some reasonable fit between technical feasibility and public acceptability. Different forms of data display, different norms, and the like should be tried. The relative credibility of the same data reported directly by a business firm and certified by an independent auditor should be explored.

Many observers believe that independent social auditing by someone such as a CPA will lack credibility. This viewpoint does not reflect the incomplete credibility of regular financial auditing. Special attention should be paid to the relative credibility of social and financial information when independently audited.

A good investigator will think of more variants than we have been able to anticipate. However, the four criteria against which they should be checked are the following: Is it believed? If it is believed, does one feel he can interpret it? (For example, a report of anti-pollution measures may be believed, but in the absence of some norm, the reader may not know what to make of it.) If he can interpret it, what conclusions does he draw from it? (A firm may meet a given norm, but the consumer of this information may or may not think this is "good performance.") Is it useful to him? (He may be able to draw firm conclusions from the evidence, but be interested in something else. He might be interested in the level of effort—true cost—while we are giving him a process audit.)

In investigating ways of reporting audits special attention should be paid to the distinction between the general public, the investing public, and the social critics of business. They are likely to use different standards.

A parallel effort should be made for audits designed for internal decision making. All the criteria suggested above would be relevant. However, in addition, one would also want to look at the effect of different auditing and reporting forms on the content of the decisions which were made.

Reporting for both public and internal use could, of course, be done with simulated data. A virtue of doing this would be to explore the necessity or lack of necessity for getting difficult-to-obtain information, such as sophisticated measures of performance. If the public were satisfied with simpler measures and confused by more complex ones, and if businessmen could make the same decisions with either, clearly the effort of getting the more complex data would not be warranted.

2. One of the key elements in the way a social audit will be received and interpreted will be the norms that are available and perceived relevant for interpreting a corporation's social performance. The norms which people prefer, and the ways in which they would use them, ought to emerge from the investigation of various ways of reporting audits suggested above. However, a separate effort should be made to identify the norms that are available for assessing the various areas of social performance, their quality, the levels of aggregation at which they are available (by industry, by region, by city, etc.), which norms ought to be available that are not, which ones might be appropriate even though the public does not presently see them as relevant, and what would be required to develop more appropriate series of norms where this would be desirable.

Some of this work is, of course, being done. Government reporting of EEO-1 reports in aggregate form by SIC category will, for many purposes, serve as norms on employment practice. The Council on Economic Priorities has developed or is developing norms of performance on various social practices for various industries. The Conference Board gathers and publishes information on corporate giving. It is intended that the work discussed here will be designed to complement what is being done by others. Perhaps special attention should be paid to the problem of updating norms developed by organizations such as the Council. Perhaps, if social auditing becomes prevalent, the development, updating, and dissemination of norms should be separately institutionalized.

3. In connection with the development of norms for social auditing, it would be worthwhile to do a number of intensive industry studies in order to understand what the special problems of social responsibility may be in a given industry and how this may vary from company to company depending on such things as the structure of the firm. When we speak of an industry we ordinarily think of a single product market, such as paper, steel, or electronics. In fact, a "company" in such an industry is highly likely to be a division of a firm that is active in several or many industries. In a given industry some businesses may be all or part of an integrated company, others may be divisions of a more complex company. (This is true, for example, of the paper industry.) This may have varying consequences for the "industry" companies. A divisionalized corporation may be sensitive to the behavior of its divisions on its overall company image, it may inject a broad point of view or a more sophisticated attitude toward technology than those of traditional firms in the industry, or it may penalize social responsibility by judging the performance of its divisions on strictly financial criteria. Variations in the location of firms within an industry may pose different problems and opportunities. For example, a firm in one community may be confronted with a large population of hard-core minority unemployed, while one in another community will have access to well educated minority group members. While the public is likely to regard such circumstances as irrelevant in making its evaluation of the social performance of firms in a given industry, most sophisticated observers will find them of relevance in judging the phenomenon of social responsibility.

What we are proposing in the way of industry studies may be viewed as a slight variant on Sater's proposal. One difference is that at this stage of the development of the technology of auditing it may be advisable not to identify specific firms. This should be left

89

to the public interest auditors. Another, and more important difference, is that the studies we are proposing would concentrate on intra-industry factors that might affect the comparability of reporting across firms within an industry.

IV. Social Responsibility within the Firm

The previous sections were concerned with the social audit *per se*. In this and the subsequent section we broaden our scope, first to a consideration of social responsibility within the firm, and then to the overall social role of the firm. We do this in the belief expressed earlier in this chapter that the corporate social audit cannot be understood apart from this broader context. The evolving social role of the firm and the problems of social responsibility within the firm will affect what is audited and how it is audited. The audit, in turn, will affect social responsibility in the firm, and presumably also affect the role which society assigns to the firm.

Business firms are, of course, the object of continual study. Yet our comprehension of how they go about and might better go about their traditional tasks is highly imperfect. In the past ten years or so our knowledge of these phenomena has been increasing quite rapidly under the impact of a new, behaviorally oriented approach. While a high portion of these studies have been done by scholars not primarily trained in the social sciences, the studies have been heavily influenced by social science methods and concepts, and would benefit from greater influence by these disciplines and a wider participation by formally trained social scientists.

This approach has generally been grounded in detailed case studies, has featured some simulation, and more recently some quantitative statistical approaches.

Our knowledge about how firms handle issues of social responsibility is much more sparse. If we view the social audit as a key mechanism in which a firm takes stock of its social performance and reports it to the public from which it in turn receives signals of approval or disapproval, then we need to understand how the corporation handles the broad issues of which the social audit may or may not become an integral part. Specifically, we need to study how the corporation perceives social policies and activities, and how it selects among the demands those to which it will respond, how it implements social policies inside the firm, and how it takes social concerns into account in the conduct of regular business decisions.

RESEARCH TOPICS.   1. There are a limited number of studies of "environmental scanning," of how a business firm gathers and processes information relevant to its regular business concerns from the outside environment. There are, to our knowledge, no systematic attempts to understand how this is done with respect to social demands and opportunities. A good beginning would be a limited number of case studies of firms whose practice may be assumed to be relatively advanced. The methodology ought to involve a comparison of the way in which social or political information is handled relative to regular business information such as that for finance and marketing. Researchers should look for: the location of the environmental sensors in the firm; the channels for reporting, and the biases and filters in these channels; the type of person doing the scanning and his perception and reception by others in the organizations, and so on.

Existing studies of environmental scanning involve no systematic use of knowledge from the field of cognitive psychology. The deliberate introduction of this point of view would enrich such studies.

Many of the difficulties that corporations have fallen into in recent times might well be viewed as organizational failures, as failures to detect, report, understand, or make correct decisions about events in the environment. These failures begin with detection and reporting. Even if the social audit matures, the problem of detecting and reporting new issues in the environment will continue to be of importance, both with regard to reactions to audit reporting and to detection and evaluation of new social issues.

2. Despite a proliferation of hortatory literature on how regular business decisions are and should be made, close examination shows that the process, more often than not, has little to do with the textbook versions. In many instances, such an examination reveals that the textbook prescriptions are not even addressed to the relevant problems. While the inquiry suggested in the preceding paragraph was directed at understanding the flow of socially relevant information from the environment to the point of decisions, it is also necessary to concentrate on the point of decision. There is little or nothing beyond anecdote to tell us how business decisions in the social area are made, although there is a good deal of business school case teaching material that can be screened for a preliminary conceptualization of this process.

There are many questions one might ask. One obvious area is a study of the factors behind the adoption of specific corporate social action. It is alleged (and acknowledged) that corporate giving is at least to some extent aimed at pleasing specific outside parties ranging from the president's wife to important customers. In addition, as we have indicated in previous chapters there are others: to satisfy personal or corporate conscience, to make the firm attractive to certain kinds of personnel, to avoid or reduce specific outside pressures, to solve social problems, for calculated business reasons (perhaps), and so on. A mere enumeration of such purposes would probably prove uninteresting. It would be of interest, however, if they had some patterned relationship to the welfare of the society or the firm or if suggestions arose from the data for a process of selection of social programs which would bring them into a more orderly relationship to the goals of the firm and the needs of society.

In addition to the motives behind the adoption of socially relevant policies, we need to understand the accompanying reasoning. How did an executive anticipate that a given action would accomplish an intended effect? How does he sort out those of his firm's actions, or those components of his firm's actions, that are socially relevant and those that are "regular business?" For example, are product policies on marketing and advertising practices seen as part of its socially responsible behavior? Is any attempt made to bring social policies into rational relationship to the firm's regular business activities? How does an executive decide what his firm can "afford?" When has an issue become sufficiently "live" to deserve attention? Is it, as in the case of one large corporation, when letters are received from some arbitrary percentage of the stockholders?

Feasible procedures for more orderly decision making on social policies should be devised and tried out. Perhaps games could be devised as training devices. Clark Abt's "Social Audit" game is such a game. Despite our reservations about the attainability of some of his objectives, it serves as a model.

3. Social responsibility like all other policies of a business firm, must be implemented through a complex organizational structure. The structure of most large firms is *very* complex. About 85 per cent of *Fortune* 500's, accounting for a very large portion of the social consequences of American business activity, are multidivisional firms consisting of a more or less tightly knit bundle of separate businesses. If the top corporate officers of such a firm decide on a social policy, how can they make it effective (or can they)? Division heads are typically rewarded on the basis of financial performance. This puts a strong pressure on divisional officers to avoid any socially responsive behavior which threatens their financial performance. Some multidivisional firms now claim to have ex-

tended their criteria for judging divisional heads beyond straight financial performance. How does this work? To what extent is this window dressing? Are there ways of compensating for the bias of the structural features of such firms?

The pattern is apt to be quite complex. We will illustrate this by drawing on some actual corporations which we know. It is possible at this point to identify three different classes of socially responsive policies each of which poses quite different problems. The first is a policy such as centralized corporate giving or released time for executives or involvement in a housing project which is under direct control of corporate officers. If the top managers are committed to such an undertaking, it is relatively easy to implement, at least in the short run, simply because it is under their direct supervision. However, the corporate staff of such a large firm tends to be sensitive about the size of the corporate budget since it is seen as an overhead drain on the divisions "which produce all the money." Corporate officers are tempted to try to assign the budget to the divisions while maintaining control over the programs at the corporate level.[18] Is this viable? What complications would it produce?

The second type of policy is one that is firm-wide, but initiated, monitored, and enforced at the corporate level. An example is a minority hiring program which assigns specific targets to each of the divisions and even to their subunits. Typically, this will be done without lowering financial targets for the divisions. Minority hiring and training programs characteristically cost money, at least in the short run, and may lower quality of service temporarily. The division heads are caught in a vise. What gives?

The third type of policy is a more general one in which top management urges a posture of social responsibility onto the divisions with the expectation that each one will respond in a way that is suitable to its particular circumstance. One may have warehouses or sales offices in a number of small communities so its involvement is through support of groups like 4-H clubs or leadership in civic enterprises of many types. Another company may be located in a number of large cities with typical urban problems. It may be developing training programs, working with the local school system, running free courses on English as a second language, rehabilitating dilapidated housing, working with minority businessmen, or cre-

---

[18] While this paper was in final preparation one of us met an official associated with public broadcasting who, unprompted by us, mentioned how difficult it was to get corporate sponsorship of public broadcast programming, because "the money is all down in the divisions and not at the corporate level, and the divisions don't want to do it."

ating a day-care center. A third may have pollution problems or product safety accusations to face. The problems of monitoring, assessing, and enforcing the corporation's broad social policy in such a situation is different from that in the first two instances. As indicated, much will depend on the "control" system that is employed, the criteria whereby the divisional officers are evaluated and the degree to which they are systematically sensitized to corporate concern in this area. In this connection we would note the Plans for Progress program, an early effort in fair employment, which failed because the top corporate leadership did not or could not transmit their concern with discriminatory practices to those down the line.

All of the above situations will exhibit themselves in modified form depending the relative power of the corporate staffs and of the heads of the divisions or affiliated companies.

Contending that corporations should be socially responsible, and proposing that a social audit be made to determine whether in fact corporations have been responsible, assumes that the corporation has the capacity to implement social policies. This is in varying degrees true, and with varying consequences for the internal life of the corporation. Hopefully, additional knowledge will suggest ways in which this implementation can be facilitated, with lessened adverse effects on the firm.

Again, accumulated knowledge on this problem in the written literature is likely to be sparse, except for general knowledge of the effects of structure on problems of control. Case studies are obviously called for.

4. Information relative to how firms take issues of social responsiveness into regular business decisions is both extensive, and diffuse and unstructured. Here we are concerned not with decisions specifically involving social problems but with regular operating decisions which may or may not have, or may or may not be perceived as having, social dimensions. Certain things are obvious. Firms that have been under fire by consumer groups, or other public interest groups, or the government will show improved responsiveness. Some firms have more enlightened leadership than others. Probably, firms in highly competitive industries are less responsive. Possibly, if some of the reasoning we introduced above is correct, the divisions of divisionalized firms may be less responsive. On the whole, however, our knowledge of that which is not obvious is scant. We might profit from a review of the existing literature (most of which will be found in journalistic reporting in newspapers and

magazines) which attempts to give some conceptualization to it.

Another approach that should be considered is that of structured case studies. One might, for example, take a particular class of decisions such as the decision to introduce a new product and study them in contexts which varied according to the competitive position of the firm in its product market and the degree and type of social pressure on it—say in regulated industries, in industries which have been under heavy consumer attack, and in industries which are neither regulated nor under consumer attack. One would expect the firms which had the most advantageous market position would be most likely to take social issues into consideration, that those in regulated industries would show a high degree of concern with a narrow range of issues, and those under consumer attack would be alert to a broad range of issues in a diffuse fashion or to a few highly selective issues if the consumer attack were highly focused. Findings which confirmed these expectations would not be highly valuable *per se*, but a study of the process whereby these firms reacted would give us knowledge of something about which we have only vague notions.

5. Contrary to popular myth, systematic long-range planning in business is not well developed. Many firms are in the process of developing such planning mechanisms. The planning systems seem to have a common developmental history in which the range of considerations taken into account gets progressively widened as the systems' capacity to handle them enlarges. A data bank at the Harvard Business School on corporate formal planning systems makes it possible to identify systems in varying stages of development. Using these data, one might identify planning systems which are likely to be on the verge of incorporating broader social issues and isolate these planning systems for case studies. It would be useful to understand how this transition takes place, what stimulates it, how the broader social data are incorporated, and how they are used. Past experiences indicate it would not be surprising if such information —even if incorporated in planning documents—went largely unused. We ought to understand why this is so.

V. *The Social Role of the Corporation*

It is obvious that the society is demanding that the corporation change its role though it is too soon to ascertain whether this shift is to be basic or simply a matter of incremental functions and concerns. This is a demand that should be made judiciously. The American corporation has shown that it can do some things very well. In the course of doing this, it may have done some things less well, and it certainly has produced some side effects that were unintended or undesirable. We are now asking the corporation to continue to do well what it did before (supply goods and services), do better what it did less well (improve product safety and reliability, afford better job opportunities to minorities and women), avoid its side effects (pollution), and additionally to help in the effort to correct many social woes to which it may have made little direct contribution, and sometimes none (offset personal disadvantages, improve educational systems, oppose governmental policies, reform transportation systems, and so on).

There are a number of risks involved. The social activities that firms undertake reflect an implicit set of priorities which result from the interaction of the social preferences of the investing community, articulate public interest groups, and corporate executives. Whether this set of priorities is the same that might come out of the normal political process is a moot question. Whether, if the set of priorities is different, it is preferable or not, is equally moot. There are those who contend that the setting of such priorities should be reserved for the political process. Businessmen, business skills, and business institutions will have distinctive contributions to make in many or all situations. But their net advantage may or may not outweigh feasible alternatives.

Some tasks might be better accomplished by other means. Whether a business executive can make a better contribution to a social program than a college professor or a trained professional is worth examining. It may be that a businessman who seeks his sense of self-fulfillment in this manner is better advised to increase the efficiency of his company so that it may produce goods or services more cheaply, or be more profitable and pay more taxes. Enjoining "business responsibility" may be less preferable than enacting and enforcing laws. This is especially true when being "socially responsible" produces a competitive disadvantage. Pollution control is an example.

Finally, we may be overburdening the decision capability of the firm. Most public discussions of the social responsibility of corporations see the main demand made on the corporation as one on its resources of money and people. This is, of course, a factor. Another factor that is seldom considered is the difficulty of corporate officers managing to maintain any coherence of effort if they try to accomplish too many objectives simultaneously.[19] The end result could be a diffusion of effort and an accompanying internal disorganization that would benefit no one.

There is a good deal of expository writing about the changing role of the corporation, and an enormous amount of reporting of business firms' responses to social demands. But there is very little analytical thinking and virtually no empirical research being directed at any of the issues we have just raised. Any program of research and development which aided the development of corporate social audits, without an accompanying assessment of the implications of what was being demanded of corporations in the way of social performance, *could* be the instrument for producing consequences that would in the long run prove undesirable. Many observers of the present scene concur in the desirability of redefining the role of the corporation. But, if this is done, it is imperative that this redefinition be evenhanded and considered.

RESEARCH TOPICS. Three types of studies are required.

1. One is a review of recent experience of business attempting to respond to social problems together with some hard thinking as to whether business is the preferred institution for meeting these needs. This inquiry should consider not only the *effectiveness of business* in solving individual problems, but also the social priorities that might be reflected in the mix of activities that result from business responding to the demands on it as suggested above.

This inquiry should be conducted by someone or combination of persons who not only understand business but the range of relevant social problems and their complexity.

2. The second type of study would concentrate on the internal consequences of business firms attempting to serve multiple objectives. The issue on which this type of study would focus is not the now familiar one of whether business firms should maximize profits or serve social purposes. It is rather the one suggested above of whether it is possible to maintain coherence of effort when a firm serves multiple objectives. Continued behavioral studies of executives grappling with these problems would be ideal.

In addition to the broad question of the overall role of the corpo-

---

[19] It is difficult to know just what form this strain on the decision structure would take. Here we have assumed that it might arise from trying to pursue several objectives simultaneously. It may also occur from efforts to respond to even one social demand on a crash basis when the signals are not clear. We have been told of such semibreakdowns of organizational processes in both the detergent and automobile industry.

ration, there is the matter of the specific issues to which the corporation is being asked to respond. From the perspective of early 1972, this appears to be a constantly evolving phenomenon. Two issues are central at this time: environmental pollution; and hiring and employment status of minorities and women. However, legislation, regulations, and enforcement proceedings are moving fairly rapidly on these two issues. It may be that within a relatively few years, the discretion of firms on these matters will be as drastically narrowed as it is in the field of labor practices, which might have served as an index of social responsiveness two or three decades ago. Performance on these issues may have little diagnostic value. Unquestionably other issues will emerge.

3. Third, the pattern of evolving social demands should be under continued scrutiny, both for their individual significance, and for their broader implications for the role of the corporations. In addition to the broad scrutiny, specific developments might be singled out for more detailed inquiry. Two current examples suggest themselves. One is the changing regulatory requirements for truth in advertising, and the generally growing notion that advertising be socially responsible. (Some of this may be reflected in the work of the newly established Advertising Review Board.) Another is regulatory pressure that T.V. programming be more socially responsive.

COMMENTS ON METHODS. The set of activities proposed here represents applied social science in a literal sense. A good deal of it is development rather than research. While a fair amount of what is involved in process audits or in ascertaining true costs would mean gaining some new knowlege, the objective is to produce a set of procedures that others may use which, in the course of use, will be successively revised and refined.

The same considerations apply to a work agenda that would extend our knowledge of such organizational processes as making decisions to undertake social programs, enforcing social policies in complex firms, and the like. They will have served their purpose if they indicate some plausible course of action which will improve organizational performance.

This means that traditional social science concepts of validity may not be applicable in the way that most social scientists usually think of it. Obviously any findings must have face validity in the sense that they are congruent with what we already know or must cause us, in some credible way, to revise what we had previously thought. That is, they must have face validity in some larger frame of reference. But the primary test of the new knowledge is its utility. Does it suggest some plausible course of action that promises improvement?

The work called for taps the skills of a variety of disciplines, and of specialties within disciplines. It would further one interdisciplinary trend already in process, namely the relating of the skills of the accountant to the more general task of organizational control. Within the traditional social sciences it calls on the methodological skills of systematic observation and experimentation, as well as the substantive knowledge of many social and organizational problems. Much of the work demands fairly sophisticated knowledge of the actual functioning of business organizations.

What is proposed here closely reflects the present state of our knowledge and capabilities apropos such phenomena as social responsibility and social auditing of business. As a result there is a call for a considerable number of case studies, a method of exploration that is particularly relevant at early stages of development of an area of knowledge. As we learn from such case studies, more systematic work of a survey or experimental nature may be called for. But this will not always be necessarily so.

Much of what we have to learn from case studies pertains to the development of models of complex organizational processes, many of which are context-determined. What one learns in one context may suggest comparable case studies in contrasting contexts. They will also suggest courses of organizational intervention that, if useful, will constitute a form of validation. Systematic large-scale study of complex social processes is an art that is very little developed, and would probably be exceedingly expensive. It is likely that in the foreseeable future the most likely and fruitful method of developing systematic knowledge of such processes will be in a complex iterative process in which the models of such processes are first checked for face validity, their context determinants specified, other case studies done in different contexts, the process models checked in practice, with earlier formulations constantly being revised under the impact of subsequent findings, and so on.

References

Abt, Clark, "Managing to Save Money While Doing Good," *Innovation*, 27 (January, 1972).

Barnard, Chester, *The Functions of the Executive*. Cambridge, Mass: Harvard University Press, 1953.

Bernays, E. L., "Emergence of the Public Relations Counsel: Principles and Recollections," *Business History Review* (Autumn, 1971).

Blum, Fred, "Social Audit of the Enterprise," *Harvard Business Review* (March–April, 1958).

Briscoe, Robert, "Utopians in the Marketplace," *Harvard Business Review* (September–October, 1971).

Bragdon, Joseph H., Jr., and John A. Marlin, "Is Pollution Profitable?" *Risk Management*, 19 (April, 1972).

Cheit, Earl S., ed., *The Business Establishment*. New York: Wiley, 1964.

Council on Economic Priorities, *Efficiency in Death*. New York: Harper & Row, 1970.

Council on Economic Priorities, *Paper Profits*. Cambridge, Mass.: M.I.T. Press, to be published.

Eels, Richard, and Clarence Walton, *Conceptual Foundations of Business*. Homewood, Ill.: Richard D. Irwin, 1961.

Feldman, Lawrence P., "Societal Adaptation," *Journal of Marketing* (July, 1971).

101

Fenn, Dan H., Jr., "Problems in Review: Business and Politics," *Harvard Business Review* (May–June, 1959).

Heyne, Paul T., *Private Keepers of the Public Interest.* New York: McGraw-Hill, 1968.

Kassarjian, Harold H., "Incorporating Ecology into Marketing Strategy: The Case of Air Pollution," *Journal of Marketing* (July, 1971).

Kozmetsky, George, "How Much Revolution Does American Business Need?," *The Conference Board Record* (March, 1971).

LaPorte, Todd, "The Context of Technology Assessment: A Changing Perspective for Public Organizations," *Public Administration Review* (January–February, 1971).

Lickert, Rensis, and William C. Pyle, "Human Resource Accounting: An Organizational Approach," *Financial Analysts Journal* (January–February, 1971).

Malkiel, Burton C., and Richard E. Quandt, "Moral Issues in Investment Policy," *Harvard Business Review* (March–April, 1971).

Mee, John F., "Profiles of the Future; Speculation about Human Organization in the 21st Century," *Business Horizons* (February, 1971).

Ohman, O. A., "Skyhooks," *Harvard Business Review* (May–June, 1955).

Oliphant, Thomas, "The New Accounting: Profit, Loss and Society," *Globe* [Boston] (May, 1971).

Public Affairs Council, "Guidelines from an Internal Corporate Social Audit—A Working Paper," Washington, D.C. (September, 1971).

Pyle, William C., "Human Resource Accounting," *Financial Analysts Journal* (September–October, 1970).